Living on the Edge

Living on the Edge

Nuu-Chah-Nulth History
from an Ahousaht Chief's
Perspective

Earl Maquinna George, B.A., M.A.

sononis
PRESS WINLAW, BRITISH COLUMBIA

NATIONAL LIBRARY OF CANADA CATALOGUING IN PUBLICATION DATA

George, Earl Maquinna, 1926-
    Living on the edge : Nuu-chah-nulth history from an Ahousaht chief's perspective / Earl Maquinna George.

ISBN 1-55039-143-7

    I. Nootka Indians. 2. George, Earl Maquinna, 1926- 3. Nootka Indians—History. 4. Nootka Indians—Biography. 5. Clayoquot Sound Region (B.C.)—History. 6. Clayoquot Sound Region (B.C.)—Biography. I. Title.

E99.N85G46 2003   971.1'2004979   C2003-905593-0

Sono Nis Press most gratefully acknowledges the support for our publishing program provided by the Government of Canada through the Book Publishing Industry Development Program (BPIDP), The Canada Council for the Arts, and the British Columbia Arts Council.

First printing: October 2003
Second printing: December 2005

Cover art, *On the Edge,* by Tim Paul
Back cover and frontispiece photo of Earl George by Robert D. Turner
Back cover photo of Clayoquot Sound by Nancy J. Turner
Maps by Robert D. Turner
Cover and interior design by Jim Brennan

Published by
SONO NIS PRESS
Box 160
Winlaw, BC V0G 2J0

1-800-370-5228
sononis@netidea.com
www.sononis.com

The Canada Council | Le Conseil des Arts
for the Arts | du Canada

Printed and bound in Canada by Houghton Boston

Contents

FOREWORD   6

ACKNOWLEDGEMENTS   11

PROLOGUE   12

CHAPTER 1   Maquinna: An Introduction   15
    The Life of the Ahousaht People   21
    My Early Years   24
    Blind Dan   28
    Tushka   33
    How This Book Will Unfold   34

CHAPTER 2   Quesahii: The People and the Sea   41
    Kista and Oo-oo-tuh, Preparation for the Hunt   52
    Ktlunoos, Seals in Nuu-Chah-Nulth Culture   61

CHAPTER 3   The Gift of Salmon   68

CHAPTER 4   Plants as Food and Medicine   76

CHAPTER 5   Naa'sQaʔitkquisHicit: Our Changing Landscape   86
    Naa'sQaʔitkquisHicit   87
    Tiskin   88
    The Beginnings of Our Nations   91
    Recollections of Fish and Forests   94
    My $13.00 Summer   99
    More on Growing Up   108

CHAPTER 6   HaHuulhi and Traditional Territories   121
    The Song of Tiskin   122
    Our Lands   127
    January 1996: The Framework Agreement   130
    February 1996: Other Resource Issues   134
    November 1996: Sovereignty   135
    April 1997: Roadblocks   138
    August 1997: A Reappraisal   141

CHAPTER 7   Conclusions   149

ABOUT THE AUTHOR   157

Foreword

Earl Maquinna George came to university at a time when most people are considering a more relaxed life in retirement. Instead, he undertook a bachelor's degree in history at the University of Victoria and then went on to graduate school to complete a master's degree there. Earl had several reasons for pursuing his academic studies. As a chief, he wanted to set an example for others, particularly the young people, to follow: to value education and to complete a difficult task. Lewis George describes his father's decision to pursue a post-secondary education: "Maquinna decided he should lead by example and enrolled in the University of Victoria [in 1990]. He often spoke with the students and always encouraged them to further their schooling. 'Any goal can be reached if you work for it,' was one of his statements to the students." At the same time, his idea was to work through the knowledge he had accumulated during his lifetime and sift out a message that would illuminate some important aspects of life on the edge. But on the edge of what? It is, of course, the edge of the vast Pacific Ocean and the west coast of Vancouver Island. But it is also the edge of two planes of existence, the edge between the white industrial world and the world of aboriginal tradition. Earl has lived in both worlds.

He has plowed through the heavy seas of his coastal homeland in a fishing boat, laboured in the relentless production line of a west coast salmon cannery, hauled big timbers out of the woods, and worked under the din and strain of the huge screaming saws of the mill at Port Alberni. He has also learned the stories and

Life on the edge: children running along First Beach at Ahousaht on sports day. This is the beach in front of Earl's house. There used to be running races along the beach, and Earl swam there in the summer.

traditions of Nuu-Chah-Nulth culture from some of his people's best historians. He has felt the healing powers of the forests and waters of his home place, and as *Ha'wiih*, has overseen and participated in the sacred ceremonies of the *tlukwana*. And he has experienced the clash between the two cultures, as when he stood in the roadblock at Sulphur Passage, barring the way of the MacMillan Bloedel loggers who came to clearcut the forests of the Ahousaht lands without the permission of the traditional First Nations caretakers of the forest lands. Industrial logging did not reflect an understanding of either the protocols of respect or the ecological and cultural implications of these actions. Earl Maquinna George has witnessed the destructiveness of logging

View of Ahousaht from the air. NANCY J. TURNER

practices on the salmon streams of the territory of which he is the keeper, and has felt the frustration of seeing the rich salmon stocks of Clayoquot Sound dwindle because of actions and forces outside his people's control.

Earl can recall events, discussions, sights, and sounds as if they happened only yesterday. For us, it has been an honour and a privilege to work with Earl Maquinna George. He is a quiet but determined man, a man of deep convictions with great pride in his heritage, a man of compassion and wisdom. He also has a sense of humour and an appreciation of character, qualities that are reflected in his stories.

Sandy beach on Flores Island, near the village of Ahousaht. NANCY J. TURNER

Earl told his family and friends at a recent recognition gathering near Coombs on Vancouver Island that one of the main reasons he pursued his university degrees was to show the younger generations the importance of education in its many forms; that it was important to set out on a task and complete it. His message was clear: if an elderly chief can do it, then so can you! It was a message of leadership and inspiration: one befitting a distinguished elder. You only needed to look at the faces of the young people in the meeting hall to see that the wisdom and strength of this message was not lost on them.

His life story, told in his own words, stands as an important record and insight into a troubled and challenging time for aboriginal peoples and their neighbours along the British Columbia coast. Although this is a written work, it is a personal recounting of events. As you read Earl's words, hear his voice and picture this distinguished elder in the presence of his family and friends. Let his deep and measured voice speak to you through these pages, because the Nuu-Chah-Nulth culture has a generations-old tradition of storytelling, passing along the wisdom gained from living on the edge.

Dave Duffus and Nancy Turner
University of Victoria
May 2003

Editors' Note on Nuu-Chah-Nulth Terminology
The Nuu-Chah-Nulth terms in this book are approximations only, using English alphabet symbols, and are not necessarily linguistically accurate.

Acknowledgements

I wish to thank many people for assisting me in bringing my story to these pages. Members of my family and the Nuu-Chah-Nulth First Nations have supported and encouraged me. I thank especially all the storytellers and relatives mentioned in the book, and all my family members, particularly Josephine George, Dawn Amos, Dr. Richard Atleo (Chief Umeek), and Tim Paul, whose beautiful artwork for the cover was done especially for this book. Thank you also to Ki-ke-in (Ron Hamilton) and Kim Recalma-Clutesi.

My friends and fellow students and teachers at the University of Victoria were also very helpful in many ways during my studies and in making this book possible. They include John Corsiglia, Juliet Craig, Dave Duffus, Diane Peacock, Gloria Snively, Nancy Turner, and Robert D. Turner.

The photos in this book are from various sources, mostly from my personal family collection. B.C. Archives is acknowledged for some of the historical photos. The two maps are by Robert D. Turner.

Finally, my sincere thanks to John Eerkes-Medrano for editorial suggestions, and to Diane Morriss of Sono Nis Press for publishing my book.

Earl Maquinna George
Port Alberni, B.C.
March 2003

Prologue

I am Earl Maquinna George. I am a Nuu-Chah-Nulth First Nations person, and the hereditary chief, as the *mamat'n'i* (outsiders, especially white people) call us, of the Ahousaht people. Europeans have called us Nootka.

In our native language, we chiefs are called *Ha'wiih*. *Ha'wiih* means something similar to, but not the same as, the Crown. We have a hereditary system of passing down the position of *Ha'wiih*, or chief, to the eldest male child in the family. Mine is a family of *Ha'wiih*, which signifies my ownership of resources, beaches, fishing grounds, forest land, and salmon streams in our home territory. Everything that is valued belongs to the *Ha'wiih*. And I am not afraid to say that these belong to me, the *Ha'wiih* of the Ahousaht territory.

The Ahousaht First Nation is one of the Nuu-Chah-Nulth nations, which include many groups of people who live on the west coast of Vancouver Island and their Makah relatives on the Olympic Peninsula of Washington State. Nuu-chah-nulth people live in the area ranging from Cape Flattery, Washington, and Becher Bay and Jordan River on southwestern Vancouver Island to the Brooks Peninsula on the northwestern coast of the island. Beginning from the south, the Nuu-Chah-Nulth peoples of Vancouver Island include the Pacheedaht (Pacheenaht), Ditidaht (Diitiidaht, Nitinaht), Ohiaht (Huu-ay-aht), Sheshaht (Tseshaht), Uchucklesaht, Toquaht, Ucluelet, Opetchesaht (Hupacasath), Clayoquot (Tla-o-quiaht), Ahousat, Hesquiaht, Muchalaht,

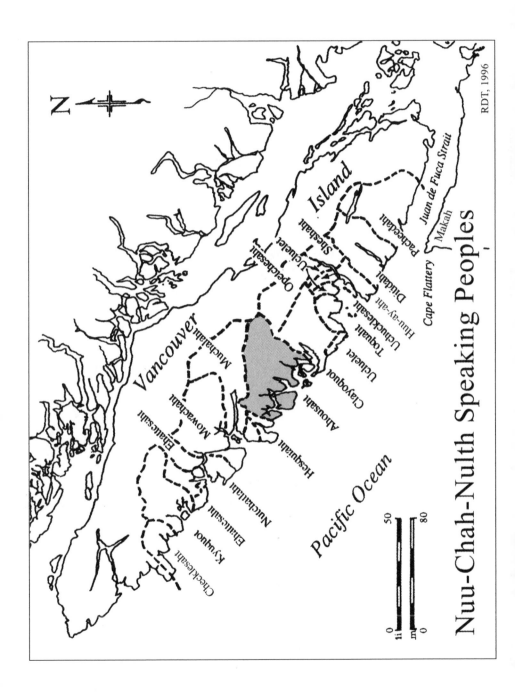

Nuu-Chah-Nulth Speaking Peoples

RDT, 1996

Vancouver Island

Pacific Ocean

Checklesaht
Kyuquot
Ehattesaht
Nuchatlaht
Ehattesaht
Mowachaht
Muchalaht
Hesquiaht
Ahousaht
Clayoquot
Ucluelet
Toquaht
Uchucklesaht
Hupacasath
Huu-ay-aht
Tseshaht
Ucluelet
Opetchesaht
Sheshaht
Ditidaht
Pacheedaht
Makah
Cape Flattery
Juan de Fuca Strait

Mowachaht, Nuchatlaht, Ehattesaht, Kyuquot (Ka:'yu:K't'h), and Chickliset (Che:K'tles7et'h').

I believe it is important to understand the Nuu-Chah-Nulth people and their relationship to the land and sea. That is my objective for this book. In particular, I will take you on an exploration of the history and environment of my home territory in Clayoquot Sound, and impart my feelings about growing up and surviving there from my own experiences and perspectives.

Growing up in a time of great change in the lives of First Nations people, I have seen and felt many things. Only a few generations before my time, the First Nations were self-governing states with our own institutions to oversee day-to-day life and the resources we depended on. Through most of my lifetime, we were treated like children by the new governors of this country. Now we are seeing the beginnings of a new period, where we can once more have control over our affairs.

There has been a great deal to think about in joining the past to the present and planning for the future of our people. This book documents some legends, recollections, and my own thoughts and feelings to develop a story that may allow onlookers to understand some of the things that are not readily apparent, especially to non-native people, about a coastal First Nation and the relationship between the people, the land, and the sea.

Maquinna: An Introduction

*Our people followed the salmon harvesting cycle, moving
seasonally to the rivers and streams in Clayoquot
Sound to catch salmon. Salmon, smoked and preserved
for the winter months, has always been our mainstay.*

I WANT YOU TO KNOW about my family and about the changes in
the structure of the village, the families, the residential school,
because these changes have much to do with our lives. It is
important for me to tell you of our movement to different salmon
streams because they are a well-known part of aboriginal people's
lives. I will discuss salmon throughout the book, and some of the
plants that have been important to us. I have also used some less
well-known aspects of our life to bring out relationships between
the Nuu-Chah-Nulth peoples and their home.

Maaqtusiis (Marktosis), the main Ahousaht village from harbour side.

Ahousaht general store, Matilda Creek — originally Gibson's.

I will start by telling about who I am and how I am able to know what I have written here. My names, Earl Maquinna George, were given to me in part through baptisms by the United Church of Canada, a church of the *mamat'n'i*. Earl comes from the title "Earl" in English royalty, and George comes from the King of England. Maquinna is a name passed down through generations of my family.

Hereditary chiefs are born with a destiny, so when they are born, they have a chief's name. At one time a wife was chosen for a chief — sometimes right from birth, sometimes later in life. I know mine was chosen for me through the high-ranking chiefs of the Keitlah family. I married Keitlah's daughter, Helen, not by my choice but by the choice of my father and my relatives. I have nine children from my first marriage — six boys and three girls. Helen died in 1976 from muscular dystrophy and pneumonia while we were away in the cold weather of Vancouver. Later I married Josephine, and as of November 2002, we have been married for 25 years.

I was born in 1926, in the village of Ahousaht on Flores Island in Clayoquot Sound. On my dad's side were Chief Billy and Chief George. They were the head hereditary *Ha'wiih* before me. It was my dad's and my own destiny to be the head *Ha'wiih* of the Ahousaht Nation. Chief Billy was a very strong person. The chieftainship meant everything to him, to be the head of the Ahousaht Nation. We are not only figureheads, but serve in the same ways as political leaders, a responsibility that is included in my translation as a *Ha'wiih* for the Ahousaht Nation. It has been my role as the head person to look after governmental work and business with other nations around the world. I act on behalf of

United Church residential school, Ahousaht. COURTESY OF BC ARCHIVES
COLLECTIONS B-01006

Residential school at Kakowis, where Earl's wife Josephine went to school.
Maybe a thousand young students went there for their school years; teachers
were Catholic priests and nuns.

the Ahousaht in undertaking various business deals as *Ha'wiih*.

My father, McPherson George, was a very strong believer in the Christian faith that he received through the teachings of the Ahousaht Residential School, which we both attended. The name "McPherson" was also given to my father by the church. At that time the missionaries thought that it was best to rename the people to whom they taught the Christian faith. My father and mother were both taught by principals, usually ministers, sent out by the missionary church from England.

The residential school at Ahousaht was run by the United Church of Canada under the sponsorship of the Government of Canada. The church funded the school and supplied the teachers and staff, the providers, who taught both Christianity and academic subjects. The reading, writing, and arithmetic were the equivalent of the standard curriculum and texts used in other classrooms throughout Canada. The first residential school was built in 1903,

Students at Ahousaht Public School, 1950. COURTESY OF BC ARCHIVES COLLECTIONS B-01009

just half a mile from my village. My father was of school age at that time and took up his education in the school. You can see that the residential school played a strong role in my personal history.

My parents married when my mother was in her early 20s. I didn't ever really get to know my mom, Mabel Davis, because I saw her slowly being troubled with illness, we believe possibly pneumonia, and probably tuberculosis. We can't really say what was wrong with her; it's just more of a guess. What we do know is that she got a really bad attack of a cold, coughing, and suffering. Being young, I didn't understand any of this, but later I did ask my dad and my aunt to fill in part of the story. My mother was a Ucluelet lady by birth, and through her there is a Ucluelet family that we were part of. My mother, and later myself and my brother Wilfred, always considered ourselves part Ucluelet. We were members of the Louie family, and there are other families that we're related to as well. My mother's father was Davis. But somehow, he moved over to Ahousaht and it was in Ahousaht that my mother's family actually lived.

Our village at Ahousaht is called Maaqtusiis, a name that means "moving from one village to another," "going from and going to," or "to stay for some length of time." The reason our village was called Maaqtusiis was that our people followed the salmon harvesting cycle, moving seasonally to the rivers and streams in Clayoquot Sound to catch salmon. Salmon, smoked and preserved for the winter months, has always been our mainstay. We travelled anywhere from five to 20 miles away from Ahousaht to fish. There were about 24 fish streams that our people relied on. The families would go and stay at a salmon stream for the season to catch the different species of salmon: chum, spring (chinook), coho, sockeye, and pink.

The Life of the Ahousaht People

Many families had makeshift houses at the salmon streams. From Ahousaht the salmon would lead us across the way from Bawden Bay or Whitepine Cove upriver towards Herbert Inlet, or up into Herbert Inlet itself all the way to the Moyeha River. We had access to all the salmon species, with enough to carry us through the winter months.

Our people used spears to catch the fish. Throughout the duration of each fishing camp, we would filet the fish, cutting into the centre of the fish, splitting off thin strips for what we call *upsl-kwi*. These smaller pieces of fish, when they dry out, are already cured and ready to eat. For larger pieces, when a whole salmon is split down the middle, they are thinned off and spread out on cedar sticks to hang up in the smoke house for at least a week until completely dry. The dried salmon is then ready for storage. All it needed was to remain in a cool and dry place, usually up in the attic at the main village of Maaqtusiis, where people had large houses, each serving quite a few families.

In earlier times, each house included one hundred people or more. Whole families lived there — men, women, and children — each of whom would have a designated spot inside the bighouse where they slept on a mat with no other flooring, even during the winter months. The fireplace in the middle of the house was where

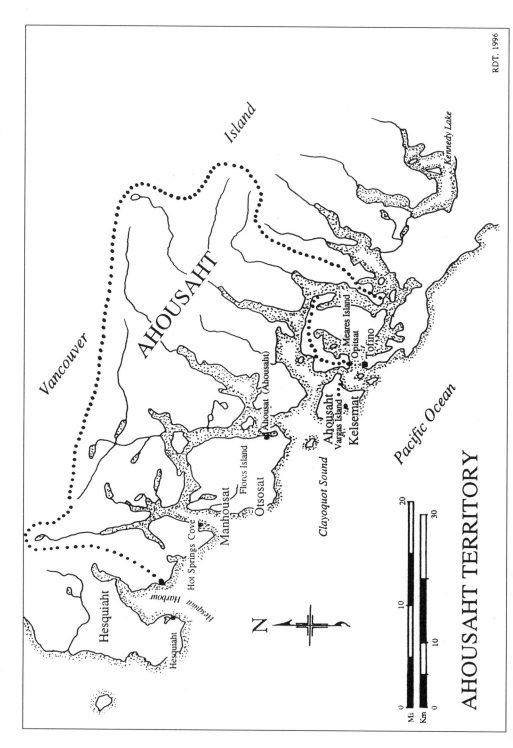

AHOUSAHT TERRITORY

RDT. 1996

22

Old growth western red-cedar; the wood is used for houseposts, canoes, and many other important items. NANCY J. TURNER

Ahousaht centre house post, Atleo's house (George Shamrock's post), where the ball field is. Later it was sold to author George Nicholson. Now it is in New York, according to Peter Webster.

people cooked and ate together. They baked salmon over the open fire and shared it with the family. There were no set meal times. People ate whenever they got hungry.

The houses were constructed of a framework of large, upright cedar timbers, which were, depending on the structure, 60 or 100 feet long and about one foot square. The timbers were hand-carved with adzes. The blades for these tools were made from sharpened stone. They had a handle of crabapple limb or other wood, which was tied onto the stone blade and rounded to make a comfortable grip.

The buildings were constructed without nails. The timbers and boards fitted into grooves and were locked together at the corners so that they wouldn't move in the wind. The siding of the buildings was made of cedar boards one to two inches thick, split with mauls and wedges. They were arranged so that they would cover the entire sides of the houses, straight up and down. At the lower end, they were buried in the sand and weighted down with piles of rocks, and then set at an angle, leaning inward to the building. The roof was framed so that boards would fit partly on top of each other, overlapping all the way down. The builders were careful to start the roof boards from the southeast end of the building so that the wind had no force over the slope of the building. The house was approximately 60 feet wide and 100 feet long, and there was a slight pitch to the roof, not too slanted, with both east and west sides equal. There were two holes towards each end of the building, at the north and south ends, for smoke to go through.

My Early Years

I did not live in a bighouse. Shortly after I was born, the bighouses were torn down and we began following the style of the people who settled in Tofino, where families made two- or three-storey buildings to house one family. When we first started building the new style of houses, the grandmothers, grandfathers, fathers, sons, daughters, and grandchildren all lived in one building until they could afford to build other houses.

No matter what type of house we lived in, the length of time we spent at an area had to do with the time it took to catch enough fish for our families. My dad's parents, and my parents too, even after spending the years in residential school, practised the same round of food gathering. The children would be cared for in the residential school while their parents were away fishing. In June, July, and August, they joined their parents at whatever stream they were camped at gathering fish. The children went back to school in September to continue their education.

The residential school children were kept at the school nine months a year and spent three months of summer holidays with their families. In my young years, I spent 12 months a year in residence because I did not have someone to live with. But I did get to know the area around Ahousaht very well in my early years. During those times there was little in the way of medical care to fight off the sickness that came about in our villages. My mother, who had been processing fish, got soaking wet and contracted a sickness that killed her early in her life. I was two years old at the time, thus I never knew my mother. Miss Chambers, a Christian missionary, nurse, and midwife, had helped my mother when I was being born. She had an interest in the health and well-being of aboriginal people. She did everything in the medical field, and after my mother died she looked after me and my brother Wilfred as a baby.

While I was at residential school, my father worked at canneries, in fish plants, and on seine boats. I and my brother

One of the famous mothers from Ahousaht – Mary Little, weaving a cedarbark basket. Her husband was William Little; they had a large family. Harold was their eldest child, and there was also Wilson, Elsie Little, and Carrie Little. Two of their grandsons are Harold and Kenny Little.

OPPOSITE PAGE:

(Above): Jessie, Queen of Keltsomaht, mother of George Shamrock, wife of Queesta, with family members.

(Below left): Dave Frank, Ahousaht, with baby. Dave was a friend of Earl's, originally from Keltsomaht.

(Below right): John Keitlah, from a big family (his brothers were all Ahousaht people who were sons of a Mowachaht lady from Nootka), with Earl's cousin, Florence Atleo. Earl married John Keitlah's niece, Helen.

Wilfred Stanley George, who was one year younger than I, were both on our own early in our lives.

I got to know many people at the residential school, since I spent so much of my early life there. We had many changes in staff. One lady was a really good cook. She knew how to make porridge and stew, and baked wonderful bread. She liked to choose from among the young men at the school to knead dough for the bread. The bread box was quite big, enough to handle 100 pounds of flour to make the dough. We were told that we had to follow the cooks' orders because they looked after the food.

Miss Alberta Reed was the missionary nurse who worked at the school. She spent her whole life in Ahousaht. She was a friend of my dad's; they could have been married, but they chose not to. Some of the accidents that happened around the school — kids getting hurt, getting cuts and bruises — Miss Reed looked after that. People came down with other ailments too. There was a time when the school had a measles epidemic, and the whole 200 kids except one, a teenage girl, were put to bed. Miss Reed and this one young girl together looked after all the 200 kids who were in sick bay. Later, a Miss Quinn came from New York all the way to Ahousaht to be the nurse, taking the place of Alberta Reed.

Blind Dan

I want to tell you how I was educated. Who were the people who taught me, and how did I learn about the things I needed to know as a boy and later as a man? When I was a youngster, I wandered around the village, visiting some of the old folks, some of whom were born in the 1860s. One of the people I spent a great deal of time with was named Dan Ambrose. We knew him as Blind Dan. He couldn't see, but somehow he knew when you were around; it looked like he could see, because his eyes were wide open. When he spoke I enjoyed listening to him. He had been a professional logger. He used to tell me, "You can't get any money sitting on your butt in Ahousaht. You get on the first boat to Seattle; you'll make lots of money." His wife used to just laugh at what the old man said. She would tell me, "He's a real big liar. Don't listen to him."

When I went to see Blind Dan, my brother would come along too. He hung around and played outside. He was a couple of years younger than me, and was not interested in sitting and talking. I could sit there all day and listen to Blind Dan. His wife was from Nitinaht, and she understood that language very well. Blind Dan picked up that language from her during their long time together. Dan's wife was a really kind-hearted person. I could see homemade bannock all over the table. She'd take that and break it and give it to us to chew on. She'd speak in her own language. I couldn't understand it, but I think I knew what she was saying. I asked Dan if he knew what she was saying, and he said, "Oh yes."

Dan was living in a logging camp on the U.S. side, and he met his woman in Seattle. He said, "One thing I learned to do was control my drinking, which was mostly wine, apple wine. It cost too much money to sit in a bar all day. All your earnings are going down the drain." He told me about just sitting in Pioneer Square, with all the people milling about. This was where he met his wife. She only had one leg. Dan wouldn't talk about what happened, but she couldn't walk, and he made a sling out of blankets and devised a way to put her into the blankets, and swing her over his shoulder like a sack. That's the way he carried his wife around in Seattle.

Dan went back up in the woods. For several years he worked in the logging industry. When we were talking, he used to ask his wife to answer some of my questions, because she understood quite a bit, but there were some things I said to her or him, and they would come back and ask me a question. Finally she would say, "I'm getting to know what you're saying." I never did get the story of how his wife lost her leg, but it may have been due to some kind of an infection. She showed me the stump once. It had fully healed. She said she had tried using crutches to get around, but she preferred to be carried by Dan. She could tell him what she wanted, what stores to go to around town. Together they lived in a hotel room close to Pioneer Square on the Seattle waterfront. Dan would go down to the docks and bum around for any kind of food he could get, usually fish heads and tails.

Blind Dan and his wife had a son, Mike, who was born in Seattle. He was just as husky as his father. By the time he was 16 years old, he'd do just like his dad, carrying his mother around wherever she wanted to go. Mike was well behaved. When he finished eighth grade at residential school, he was given permission to stay on for another year to do chores. Every morning in the summer, when my brother and I woke up at five or six o'clock, Mike would be down at the water already.

Mike was a very polite person, really artistic and knowledgeable. He made his own canoe. When his family was in Ahousaht, his life was at the residential school. Each morning, he'd come and see how his mom and dad were, and after that he'd be on the fishing grounds in his canoe. People could see in his canoe the work of an artist. He made it without any plans, using just a knife and an adze. He fished around most of the local islands and reefs on the outer side of Flores Island, Sea Otter Rock, Bear Island, and close to Rafael Point.

Mike drowned. Or at least they figure he drowned. It was summertime and they found his canoe not far from Flores Island, the south end, Long Beach. The canoe fishermen fished close to the rocks there, where the salmon came by. Mike must have left real early in the morning. We saw the prints of his canoe on the beach that day where he dragged it down the beach. He must have taken his shoes off, because they were still sitting on the beach. He had forgotten to put them in the canoe. No one really knows what happened to him. The men in other canoes that were around found the canoe, just dry, with no water in it. They had no way of knowing what had happened.

It was kind of sad, because Old Blind Dan didn't get along well with his son. They quarreled a lot, mostly about Mike not staying home, choosing to live in the residential school. But Dan got very suspicious when Mike died. It came to his mind that his son might have been murdered. He went to one person and said, "You murdered my son." People didn't really want to hear such accusations. They didn't know what had really happened, but he did not believe them.

People went to tell him, "No, Mike fell overboard. He had a heart attack or something." But Mike was gone. And Dan's wife ended up in Essondale Hospital, a psychiatric hospital. The RCMP took her away.

As for Blind Dan, well, off and on he'd want to talk to people, so I kept listening. He was right from Ahousaht. Dan came from a family who were from the house of my grandparents and my dad, the bighouse named *Lhep hayachiisht*: that's the words naming the Thunderbird that came down, and its wings were slowly going down as he landed. That was the name of our bighouse, my dad's, my grandfather's, and the other parts of the family, sisters and brothers, Dan too was part of that house. Dan's native name also indicated where he came from. Nobody else could use that name, even take that name.

One of Dan's ancestors was responsible for killing Kaanaqim the giant, another prominent story in our history. Dan's ancestor challenged Kaanaqim to a duel and Kaanaqim said, "I'll take you all on, and you'll be out of my misery, you'll be dead before you reach the door." Two years from the time they started to plan to kill Kaanaqim, he was dead, at the hands of Blind Dan's ancestor, one who was called Betokamai, and another, Totohasta.

Dan was very knowledgeable; he knew a lot about his background, his history. I looked after him in his last years. He'd make an order out to the grocery store, Huey Clark's general store, which is still there today. The first thing he put on his order was one slab of bacon — one whole slab. He could down that in one meal.

I'd always see him at the feasts in the winter months. Those feasts were Blind Dan's favourite, he could eat lots. Our people were quite strict about how the feasts were carried out. Each person had his own seat, and no one else could have that seat. The women were on the other side, and they did their duties as to what songs and chants were presented. They fixed the food, crabs and certain other delicacies, sea urchin, all the different things that grow on the rocks. They'd get a lot of abalone too. There isn't anything that our people didn't use. There were oysters to be had, but oyster wasn't a delicacy. Oysters are good for the soul, that's what they said.

Dan was like my grandfather, and he liked me. He talked quite a lot. He knew every part of my family and he knew and respected how we became the hereditary chiefs.

Tushka |

There was another old man called Tushka, who I remember well from my childhood. He had a cane, and at all our feasts, after the dinner was eaten, he got up and banged his cane on the floor, and in this way he was the start of what was to go on. He announced what the feast was for and who it was for. He always started with the history of where our people came from. Tushka must have been one of the leading historians of our culture. He knew about the songs and the dances that go with each family.

Tushka was not only interested in the Ahousaht people; he also knew a great deal about the Keltsomaht relationship and how we were linked to other tribes, mostly by being close relatives to the hereditary chiefs of Keltsomaht, hereditary chiefs of Manhousaht, and various *Ha'wiih,* throughout the different communities. There were tribes that were together with each other, inside Bedwell Sound, Warn Bay, Cypre River, Meares Island. Those relationships have a history, all by themselves. This is what Tuskha used to talk about, how things came about: the ownership of all the beaches and the land, the resources. There was a lot to do with forests, fishing grounds, halibut banks, codfish banks, salmon banks.

At the feasts there were several other people who spoke, and it would become a long, drawn-out day, going well into the evening, when these knowledgeable people talked for hours at a time. Many people did listen to them, and those were the ones who learned well. They are the ones who know the Ahousaht and Nuu-Chah-Nulth history today, the history that Tushka brought out.

Young children had a hard time trying to understand what Tushka was saying; their real questions came later at home. You wanted to know what Tushka had been talking about — the Ahousaht people and the confederation of Keltsomaht, Manhousaht — the places, Warn Bay, Bedwell Sound, Meares Island, Cypre River. The story of Kaanaqim that I mentioned earlier, and of Kaanaqim's claim to get rid of all the hereditary chiefs and take over as the chief of all the tribes. Tushka and the other historians knew all the place names that had been around for thousands of years. They also had full knowledge of where all the valuable resources were, such as the fishing grounds, and on the land, where a deer or two would be quite easy to get during those times.

How This Book Will Unfold

Now I will begin with the story of how my people came into possession of the lands and waters they now have. I will then tell you about the life cycle of early Nuu-Chah-Nulth hunters, focusing on the story of pelagic fur seal hunting and the influence that the Pelagic Sealing Treaty of 1911 had on us. I will tell you the story of hunting seals and of expert seamanship using dugout canoes in the fur seal migration path as far away as 50 miles offshore from Vancouver Island.

My story about the fur seal hunting continues into the early days of the pelagic sealing industry that became available to the Nuu-Chah-Nulth tribes. People from all the tribes were hired, signed articles, and brought their canoes, their shotguns, rifles, ammunition, and enough food for the long days when the sealing schooners followed the seals in the northern hunting grounds. The time spent away from home could be as long as nine months of the year. Some people became wealthy as seal hunters, but some were barely able to make a living.

After I present some historical discussion, I will come back to the present, the 1990s and the new millennium, to the modern treaty process, in particular, to questions of our lands, resources, and rights. The first part of the first day of the first presentation made by Canada in these treaty talks stated that there would be no compensation for wrongdoing made by either government entering the treaty process, Canada or British Columbia. Furthermore, we were told there would only be five percent of the land base available for the return of traditional lands to First Nations. Recently, the Nisga'a Tribal Council farther north have finished negotiating their treaty. They have gone through the modern-day treaty process of starting with a framework agreement, and from that going to an agreement-in-principle, and, as of 1999, their treaty has been signed and ratified. The Nisga'a Treaty outlines settlement of land, settlement of resources, and settlement of the question of self-government.

The problem with these modern-day treaties is that there is

strong opposition in the political arena. New voices are being heard from people, third-party interests, that are not agreeable to settling the land question with First Nations in British Columbia. Two political parties, the Reform Party and the Liberal Party, are saying to the First Nations that there is "one law for all" and that there should be equal access to ownership of land by purchasing land rather than having it returned to its original owners, the First Nations. I find this particularly ironic as we First Nations have lived under a different law imposed upon us through the Indian Act for the better part of the century.

The fact is that people seem to have a very biased perception of what is going on in these negotiations. They do not recognize some of the things that occurred with the colonization of British Columbia. We had a system of government and laws for our people at the time of the Royal Proclamation of 1763. Europeans simply used the British North America Act of 1867 to gain control of the land that was not settled or did not appear to be settled or occupied by European standards. It is sad and very unfair for decisions regarding ownership of properties in large tracts of land all across Canada to have been made in Britain and imposed on us, without our voices being heard.

I have already stated that we have opposition from third parties who I think have no say whatsoever in the settlement for our lands. They are standing on land that they gained by bullying and coercion. Although there was no war, there was an attack by the British navy on the Ahousahts. The Ahousahts sank the British vessel *Kingfisher*. In return, in 1864 the British navy bombarded the Ahousaht and the other communities in the area in order to punish them for sinking the *Kingfisher*. We considered the *Kingfisher* an alien, as other settlers had already taken land away from other Ahousaht people on Vargas Island. The Ahousahts naturally saw the same intentions of the people on the sailing vessel *Kingfisher*. The British Navy destroyed 60 of our canoes, which were vital to our day-to-day life.

This was not a war. We consider it punishment for the Ahousaht Nation. We retaliated and fought back and the British backed down. According to our history they killed over 100 people, but they did not have to account for how they plundered the Ahousaht people. It was merely called a punishment. They wrecked the houses and canoes and took as hostage a chief, or *Ha'wiih* youngster, called Keitlah Mukum. He was the hereditary second chief of the Ahousaht Nation. The English warship *Sutledge* was anchored out near Opitsaht after the bombardment of the villages near Tofino. The Tla-o-qui-aht chief, Wickanninish, made an offer to the captain of the English warship for one sea otter skin to release young Keitlah Mukum. The captain accepted, and the British ship returned to Esquimalt.

Not only were our government and peoples plundered, but the newcomers took without permission from the traditional resources of people living in Clayoquot Sound. Those resources are the same ones that were eventually handed over to corporations like MacMillan Bloedel (now Weyerhaeuser), Interfor, Canadian Pacific Railway, and I could name many others that gained favours from politicians inside the government of British Columbia, giving them the right to harvest and own land that belonged rightfully to First Nations.

In 1997, we won a little piece of what was ours in an interim measures agreement. For three years, for the tribes from Central

Region, Clayoquot Sound, this agreement has stated that we are to regain land which is rightfully ours. We are here to regain authority over the many resource holdings that are in Clayoquot Sound, meaning beaches, salmon spawning beds, resources on forest land, and all the things that we have not yet negotiated through the interim measures agreement, which was extended in 2000.

The story that unfolds is entirely a personal narrative. I use no outside sources other than my own recollection of events, stories, and legends. While I am aware of the ethnographic accounts, the compilations, and the reconstructions done about us by outsiders, they have a flaw that makes them a different kind of work than I have done here. The work of a non-native is coloured by the inability of the outsider to experience the context of the information collected. Although scholars believe they know all about us, there are many parts of native life that have never come out in their work. When I read that material, it simply has no character and is not authentic, and some of it is plain wrong.

Part of the reason for the lack of understanding in the writings about us is that for much of the time we have existed under the control of the Indian Act, which we believe prevented us from discussing our culture. We believed that to do so would land us in jail. Whether or not such a law exists is not the issue; the point is, we believed that was the case. The entire story of our people exists as a large body of information carried in our memories, sometimes with conflicting details between families, but always subject to the same sorts of forces that shape our culture. It is an ongoing conversation among the people.

Still today, material is being taken from us under a variety of disguises and is used against the people. Recently, detailed ethnographic work was done at the behest of a multinational forestry corporation that may end up working against our treaty settlement, and that work is no better than the rest of the incomplete story compiled by outsiders.

The difference with the information herein is that I decided the agenda and the order of the information, and in some ways that is a shortcoming. Documentation by outsiders is an artifact of the order and the orderliness of western cultures; it is not a part of our way of knowledge. It is hard to write about myself. Maybe I am bitter about people writing about us, about me, rather than creating a picture as I see it. There is a real difference, and I feel it is important enough for me to write this not so much to set the record straight, but more to provide an example of what my world is like.

I have no list of interviews and have never "collected" information. My information has been assembled over the past 70-some years. From the time I was a small child I have heard stories from my family, my friends' families, and aboriginal people from many places. There is still much information in my thoughts, images of fur seal skins piled on the dock, the "one-lunger" engines starting up before sunrise, being hauled into a courtroom in Port Alberni, charged with violating fisheries regulations for exercising my aboriginal right to hunt for food. Some of that is included here, and some of it is not. Perhaps that is a flaw of the book; parts are not always linked, and it is not bound together in a continuous story. However, that is the way the information exists and has since time began for us. We lived here long before Franz Boas, Gilbert Sproat, the many Indian agents and band managers, treaty negotiators, fishing companies, logging companies, and government agents, as surprising as that may seem to non-native people.

My book, which is based on my master's thesis at the University of Victoria, is not in the usual form of scholarship that university degrees are based on. However, I think it is a valid form for presenting my thoughts for many reasons, particularly because it seeks to build understanding of First Nations. A better understanding of First Nations is important for reasons of justice in land and resource settlements, for better understanding of the many cultures in Canada, and for providing a different look at the way people and the environment coexist.

Quesahii:
The People and the Sea

*The generations of Nuu-Chah-Nulth people younger than
me have no memory of the seal meat and pelts, nor of the
precarious journey to offshore waters in small boats.*

THIS CHAPTER SPEAKS OF PEOPLE and marine animals and their place
in the resource base of the Nuu-Chah-Nulth of the west coast. It
begins with a story that relates some of the history of the Ahousaht
and the way we secured the lands we now have as part of our
traditional territory. We came to take possession of the salmon
streams and other waters that we now claim, after a war which
took place in the last century. I will also tell of two specific cases
of how marine animals were vital to our survival. Hunting the

large whale is an important topic because whales now are very important to non-native people as well. Our history also includes fur seal. Our history of fur seal hunting is one example of the changes that were imposed on the Ahousaht people as part of our relationship with newcomers.

Two people helped me put this story together at different times through my life. My grandfather, Peter Webster, was a learned man who helped to develop the linguistic understanding of our language at the University of Victoria and at the Provincial Museum (now Royal British Columbia Museum). He told me some of what I am going to tell you about the history of Atleo River area. John Jacobson, another Ahousaht historian, also gave me much information that he learned from his father and the elderly people of his family. John used to call me in the middle of the night and he would say, "Did you know this?" and I would say, "Know what?" "Well, this story I've been trying to tell you." And he'd tell me part of a story and then the telephone would abruptly hang up. He never finished telling me all of the stories. In these next sections when I discuss the term "owned," I am referring to a concept we call *HaHuulhi*.

Long ago, in the latter 1700s and into the 1800s, the entire area around Atleo River belonged to a people called the Otsosat Nation (see map on page 22). They owned all of Flores Island, all the rivers and streams that cross Flores Island, Bawden Bay, White Pine Cove, and Herbert Inlet, all very rich in salmon. And every year the different species of salmon came at their own times to spawn. Up in the Moyeha River, in Herbert Inlet, there were pink salmon we call *ch'ap'i* — really good eating fish, lean and light in colour.

The Otsosat also owned the Atleo River, which was one of the richest rivers at that time. Year after year the chum salmon came by the thousands into that stream. They laid their eggs in the fine gravel beds. In my own time I can remember seeing the female chum salmon using their tails to dig into the gravel to lay their eggs. Nature, knowing how to create a hatchery, brought in the male fish that laid the milt, turning the stream almost white.

As I stated earlier, the Atleo River belonged to the Otsosat Nation. It was a big tribe that may have had as many as 10,000 members. Each one of those rivers belonged to certain families from the Otsosat Nation. That includes a stream that I named Shark Creek (called McGregor Creek on the maps and charts). In our language the place is named after *mamach-aqtlnit*, the great basking shark. They resemble *yacha*, the dogfish, but they can reach 40 feet long. When we were teenagers, we would see the shark come up out of the deep water down on the floor of the Millar Channel and swim with a fin on top of the water, and we would go alongside in our boats.

The basking shark went into Shark Creek on the high tide, up over the gravel bar into that creek and into a pool below a set of falls. It would hide underneath the falls and bear its young. My grandfather said that the shark knew where to go in order to have its young and be safe, be free from other predators. So they said this animal, this great big shark, has a knowledge of that special spot called Mamach-aqtlnit.

The Otsosat owned the whole of the area designated by an imaginary line from the south side of Catface Mountain, to a point halfway from Hot Springs Cove to Hesquiat. They would not allow any other tribe to come past that boundary. If anybody did pass without permission, they killed them or chased them away. They were not a friendly tribe.

At one time they made the mistake of murdering someone from the Ahousaht tribe. I am not sure how the killing took place, but a war erupted from this event. It began as a small conflict. The Ahousaht knew who the killer was because they had knowledge of most of the Otsosat families. The same knowledge is still here: someone living in Ahousaht, or in Tla-o-qui-aht, or someone living on this side of the Clayoquot Sound; most everybody knows each other. Part of that knowledge is through the intermarriage amongst people all through the Nuu-Chah-Nulth or west coast people. The people of the Otsosat Nation were married to Tla-o-qui-aht, Ahousaht, Mowachaht, and Hesquiaht people. Somewhere around 1800, the war began to grow more fierce. There were raids, night raids that killed as many as 80 to 100 people in one night. Guns bought from fur-dealers were given to the Ahousaht tribe from the Mowachaht people because of family ties. Many Mowachaht women were married to high chiefs in Ahousaht. However, there was also intermarriage of Mowachaht with the Otsosat Nation, making alliances difficult.

The Mowachaht got their guns from the European sailing ships that anchored outside of Friendly Cove and in through the area where Mowachaht, Ehatisaht, and Kyuquot peoples were living. For a long time, Europeans used to go by on the sailing ships but were unable to land because of the big waves and rocks. The Nuu-Chah-Nulth helped the sailing ships to find deep passages to come in and anchor, and through that they gained access to Friendly Cove and Esperanza Inlet.

At that time the Ahousahts were living on Vargas Island and

up into Cypre River, Bedwell Sound, some on Meares Island, Keltsomaht, and the outer islands, abiding by the borderline at Catface Mountain. Ahousahts had already formed a confederacy with the Keltsomaht, and the tribes that lived in Bedwell Sound, the Quatsweaht. They were also 10,000 strong.

Chief Maquinna, of Nootka Sound, Earl's ancestor. Madrid Atlas, 1802; plate #12; ca. 1800. COURTESY OF BRITISH COLUMBIA ARCHIVES A-02678

But the war was not an everyday war. It was guerrilla warfare, where there were raids from either side. In this conflict the Tla-o-qui-aht, neighbours to the immediate south, were neutral, although they wanted to see the Ahousaht lose the land as they thought Tla-o-qui-aht would thus gain property on their own boundary with the Ahousaht. They were kind of enemies, but again, intermarriage was quite strong and family sided with family.

John Jacobson related much information to me about the warriors — their reputations for bravery, how they fought, and how they survived. He told me the story about Maquinna (also written as "Mukwina"), my direct ancestor; my blood and name flow from Maquinna. He was a warrior who survived because he had a true honest slave. Not a slave in the way African people were to the white people, more like a trusted servant. This man looked after Maquinna. When Maquinna was sleeping, this man was awake. He had his guns ready in case somebody attacked during the night. And they did a lot of hiding during the daytime, when it was dangerous to go in the open.

War plans were made on top of Catface Mountain, from where they could see the land on both sides. The planners of this war looked mainly at the rivers: all the rivers and streams draining into the Millar Channel on the Otsosat side. There were not many rivers on the Ahousaht side, the Cypre River being the only major stream on this side in our territory. We were limited in our access to salmon. There were small rivers on Vargas Island producing a few cohos each year, but no chums. We only got a few chums at Kakawis on Meares Island, in Bedwell Sound and Warn Bay. Most of the good salmon rivers were in the Otsosat territory.

So a warrior, Haayuupinulh, who my son Bill is named after, sat on that mountain with a gathering of 40 warriors. They were all speaking, one at a time.

Haayuupinulh said, "I'll start the war, and I'll swear that I'm going to kill all Otsosat on that side. That is going to be my will in my life." And he said, "You don't have to join me because of the many reasons that you as warriors have. I know you have blood relatives over there. You have uncles, aunts, cousins, close relatives married in the Otsosat Nation." Maquinna decided not to participate. He said, "I'm going to stay neutral. I have blood relatives there. I'll see how you do. I'm not afraid to fight. I'm not afraid to join the war. I am on your side, but I will not fight because I want to see how the war progresses or whatever will happen. They can come and kill me and I'll protect myself but I

The mouth of the Megin River, one of the special areas of the Ahousaht Nation. NANCY J. TURNER

will not go over and kill anyone on that side of that line."

But all of the 40 that were at that meeting on top of Catface Mountain joined forces with Haayuupinulh. Looking at the 10,000 people and the God knows how many warriors there were on the Otsosat side, they were brave men. They swore that they would protect and fight for each other until the last. The fight was not every day or every night. It went in spurts. There was no special time, although the Otsosat Nation figured out that the Ahousaht attacked according to the phase of the moon.

In order to fight, a warrior had to be prepared in terms of his spirituality, his protection from being killed, and the medicine that he used was strong in his body, inside and out. They prepared for the war through *uusimch* (cleansing and praying), through swimming in a bathing pool, something like the one at Shark Creek. There were streams and pools all through the inlets and on the islands. The people who were on the islands bathed in the salt water. But the ones living near the Bedwell and Cypre Rivers bathed in the river. Bathing was a cleansing: cleansing of the soul, cleansing of the body, cleansing of the mind, cleansing of evil spirits. And it was exchanged for the strong will to live and fight.

Two years from the time the war started, Maquinna's brother was killed on the beach at Kutkous, where the Otsosat Nation built a wall out of cedar poles stuck into the sand leaning outward so that it could not be climbed. It was a protection from attack by the Ahousaht. The warriors had no fear because the belief was: "I am not going to die. Nothing can kill me." Maquinna's younger brother was killed by a shot. He was walking slowly up the beach, and he had a gun in his hand. A stray bullet hit him and killed him. It was ironic because the gun of that day was very poorly made. Instead of the shot going straight, it was carried in an arc. That's the way the barrel of the gun was made, poor guns from poor gunsmithing. The guns were made in Europe.

So the warriors used to laugh. They'd say, "I can see that bullet. See the way it curves? Nobody can kill anybody with one of those poor guns. I'd rather kill a person with my knife, or my spear, or my club." It was not a joke, because they knew what the gun was like; but it was called *ta-kliulth*, meaning "shooting straight."

Upon hearing that his younger brother had died from a gunshot wound, Maquinna went to take him home to Vargas Island, to where they were living on the outside in Ahous Bay, and there he buried him. Maquinna had previously stated he would not enter the war, that he would be neutral, but his new position was, "I'm going to step over your body, your dead body, my brother, because I'm going to now enter this conflict, this war. You're gone, I'll be here. I'll fight until the last person is killed on our enemy side. And I vow vengeance for your death." This is the story from John Jacobson.

That marked the beginning of Maquinna's participation in the conflict. Two years after the meeting on Catface Mountain, he entered the fight. Haayuupinulh himself died two years after that meeting on the mountain, by an enemy spear. Once he entered the war, Maquinna and his slave travelled in enemy territory and killed many people. Maquinna was hated, and the enemy vowed that one day they would find him and kill him for all that he did to the tribes of Otsosat Nation. John Jacobson related that Maquinna killed as many people as the best of the warriors that fought over approximately 15 years.

The Otsosat Nation started to back away from the war. The Ahousaht were saying that they were not going to spare any Otsosat. The Otsosat response was, "We may as well find shelter somewhere or move a long ways away so that at least we'll live.

The brave Ahousaht warriors like Maquinna are not going to spare any one of our people. They're going to kill every one of us, right to the end."

Before the Otsosat Nation was completely exterminated, some fled south. They showed up in places like Tacoma and Seattle in Puget Sound on the American side, and on the outer coast, on the Olympic Peninsula, at Neah Bay. In later years they showed up singing songs, the same songs that came from their tribe. So, the Ahousaht knew that they survived and pursued some of them as far as Neah Bay. They told the Neah Bay people, the Makah, "You give us the Otsosat people. If you don't, we'll kill you too." So the Neah Bay people killed the Otsosat refugees and gave the heads to Ahousaht. The Neah Bay people feared the Ahousahts.

It does look like Maquinna married more than once. I do not know the story about his first wife. My bloodline comes from Maquinna and his marriage to a woman from the highest chieftainship of the Tla-o-qui-aht Nation, a lady of royalty. Around this time, Maquinna settled at the Atleo River. He said, "I choose this spot as my new homeland because of the richness of the fish going up that river, because of my contribution to our war, our Ahousaht war, with Otsosat Nation." So Maquinna built a house and started a family at the mouth of the Atleo River, right on that green spot that can still be seen today. Thus the Ahousaht came to their new territory as spoils from the war. The rivers and streams were divided among the victors. A large part of it was given to Maquinna, as *HaHuulhi*. Maquinna took Megin Lake, Megin River, Shelter Inlet. I don't know when Atleo River became the *HaHuulhi* of Atlieu, representing the line of Chief Richard Atleo now. But somehow that is how the division of property and land was given, including water rights, the foreshore rights, and offshore rights.

Both John and Peter told me about Maquinna and his new territory. Maquinna was in bed resting with his new wife, the Tla-o-qui-aht woman. His slave came into the house and said, "There's enemy canoes on the beach. You'd better wake up and get ready and go. I don't know how many of them there are." Maquinna donned his clothes, put on his weapon, and he went through the back way up the river. By that time, Otsosat warriors were already in the house and they had already killed his wife. Maquinna was mistaken in his belief that the whole of the Otsosat Nation were killed. He relied on his slave to take care of his wife. But the Otsosat had killed her. Maquinna hid in the brush up the river while the Otsosat searched all over for him. They were going to gain their vengeance, and for that purpose they had grouped together to kill Maquinna, but they did not find him that day at Atleo River.

Maquinna fled north, up the Atleo River he went, through the higher part of the hill, and came down on Shark Creek, to the waterfall. The Otsosats, fearing more Ahousaht would return, pulled away. There was quite a few Otsosat left yet, I guess, even after Maquinna had already claimed Atleo River.

The Tla-o-qui-aht Nation heard of the death of their queen. And they heard that it was Otsosats who killed her. So they put all their canoes together, all their warriors together. They went and they finished the Otsosat Nation off, hunting them down all through their hiding places. The Tla-o-qui-aht are the ones that actually finished the war, in a state of vengeance for their queen and my ancestor, my grandmother.

Through this war the Manhousaht people who were living in Hot Springs Cove and Hisnit between Hesquiat and Hot Springs Cove were spared, although they were part of the Otsosat Nation. The Ahousahts spared them on account of the many close relationships between the tribes. In return, the Manhousaht gave up all their rights and the land on that side, which was given over to Haayuupinulh's family in settlement. John Jacobson's own family had a place called Utla-Kutla, a coho river across from Hot Springs on the northwest side of Flores Island.

Much of the traditional land holdings of the Ahousaht date from this war. Access to many important resources — good cedar trees, salmon streams, herring spawning beds, and whales and seals — resulted from this war.

Kee-sta and Oo-oo-tuh, Preparation for the Hunt

Two or three generations after the Otsosat war, Kee-sta Atleo and many young warriors were heirs to the settlement lands of former Otsosat territory, including Bartlett Island, called Nu-a-suk, seaward on the southwest side of Flores Island. Kee-sta was the third hereditary chief of the Ahousaht Nation, which ranked him down from the Keitlah Mawhim, who was second by rank. He was known for his spearing skills. This story, however, relates to Kee-sta's ability to spear and catch a whale and the long preparation for this hunting of the whale.

Kee-sta Atleo pledged to go and hunt and kill a whale. It was his ambition to do what seemed impossible. There were other

MacKay Island, a culturally important landmark of Clayoquot Sound.
NANCY J. TURNER

hunters from the Ahousaht tribe on Nu-a-suk. Another hunter was Xiyiks, also known as Ahousaht Amos. He was another of the ambitious young men dedicated to hunt the big whale. There was another hunter besides Kee-sta and Xiyiks. The man was also Ahousaht; I know his daughter was Nellie Jacobson, but I do not know what his Indian name was. These were the three hunters who were given the task of capturing and killing the whale for the Ahousaht Nation. They settled on Bartlett Island and spent two years talking to the Creator on the task of capturing and killing a whale.

When captured, the whale was cut up into sections that were

given to the hereditary chiefs: Maquinna, Keitlah, and Kee-sta. The hereditary chiefs took his heart. The other part, which was on the left side of the whale, was given to Keitlah. Kee-sta, as the man who had killed the whale, took the next part of the whale, which held the very rich pieces of meat and blubber, and he also got the head and tail. And all the Nuu-Chah-Nulth Nation, from one end of the island to the other, were invited to come and celebrate the capturing, killing, and towing of the whale into Nu-a-suk (Bartlett Island). Eventually, all the parts of the whale were given away in a ceremony, and people from many parts of the coast were rejoicing and feasting. The most useful part of the whale was the blubber, which was smoked. The meat and blubber were smoked to give it flavour. There was no part of the whale that was not used.

The type of whale hunted by these young hunters, the *ma7ak* (grey whale), is also called *iih tup* because it is large. They were the largest mammal in the area. *Kaka7wi'n* (killer whale) was not hunted because it was known to be a sacred type of life that had the power to go on the dry land and then be part of a wolf family. There are stories that say that the killer whales travelled on land across to lakes. The ability to turn back into a killer whale was a sacred power. So the respect for that entity meant that it was not used for food purposes. There are many stories of this happening, and special people were known to have seen this transformation happen to the killer whale.

There were good and bad happenings during the time of the *oo-oo-tuh*, the preparation for the killing and spearing of the *iih tup*, the big whale. There is a story about Ahousaht Amos. He was going for his daily bathing in a sacred pool on Nu-a-suk. There was an incident when Nellie Jacobson's father was found dead in the pool that belonged to Ahousaht Amos. There was suspicion that her father was murdered while inside the pool that belonged to Ahousaht Amos. The rules and ownership rights were very distinct, and it was not a good omen to bathe in someone else's pool. The belief was that if you did not kill the person inside your pool, you would have bad luck all the rest of your life. These happenings were only one generation earlier than mine.

This was the thought that was brought out when Kee-sta captured and killed one whale that was towed to Nu-a-suk. Ahousaht Amos got two whales killed, captured, and towed onto Nu-a-suk.

On each of these occasions, the killing of the whale and the division of the food was done in the traditional way. People from all the Ahousaht Nation and farther away gathered to come and enjoy the celebration and feast of the killing of the whale. There were Kwagiulth people from the other end of the Island; Nimpkish Lake people came to attend the ceremony of the killing of the whale and enjoy the feast that was put on. Also, people from Neah Bay, Washington. Of course there were famous whale hunters from all the Nuu-Chah-Nulth Nations that took part in that. People of the Ohiat (Huu-ay-aht) First Nation attended with all their famous hunters, who were well known for hunting and killing the giant whales. Many people came to take part in that ceremony which made Kee-sta Atleo a very famous man.

Vital in the preparation of a hunt was also the carving of a whaling canoe. This giant canoe was over forty feet long and six feet in width, carved to a sharp point at the bow with a gradual slope to the stern end. The boat needed extra depth to give it

A grey whale off the west coast of Vancouver Island.

A dugout canoe. The man standing beside the canoe is probably David Frank, a canoe builder.

Tutsuhp (sea urchin) captured on a spear – a delicacy enjoyed by west coast people.

The late John Jacobson, a war veteran and storyteller.

balance to allow a pair of oarsman, one on each side, to work. This made room for eleven hunters, including one at the stern acting on the rudder to manoeuvre and head off the whale. There is a difference between these whaling canoes and the canoes that are made for other purposes. There is a special shape to the bottom and the upper sides of the canoe. Whaling canoes flared up to the bow, and the stern was made especially for manoeuvring and following the whale on the hunt. They were built very smoothly, with carving around the bow and the stern ends. In the bow, the carving of the thunderbird faced upward, with the wings spanning towards where the width grew. They were coloured with engravings of a spearman, a whale, and a thunderbird on the sides of the canoe.

The canoe was dug out of a cedar log with a special hand adz called *chuhyak*. An especially sharp twin-bit axe was used to dig the inner part of the canoe. The cedar log itself had its own history, being taken from a high level on the slopes of a place like Catface Mountain. There were several canoes that were made up there, and also in Ross Passage behind MacKay Island was a special place for some of the canoes. Some other canoe logs were taken from Moyeha River; along the high ridges we find the remains of where canoes were dug out until they were light enough to drag down to the ocean. When the initial forming was finished, the canoe was towed to Bartlett Island to finish carving and preparing it to give it the well-balanced hull needed for the whale hunt.

These giant canoes were seaworthy. On the Pacific coast winds flare up in a very short time. In one or two hours the winds can develop stormy conditions which make the ocean dangerous. As well as being seaworthy, the boats were also quiet and manoeuvrable. The paddle played a very strong role in a stealthy approach to a whale. The paddle was sharp on the end and had a handle to fit into the palm of either hand. And when the paddle hit the water it made less sound so as not to alert the whale, which could hear movement in the water. The whale knew where the hunters were at all times.

This time, when Kee-sta killed the whale, it surfaced at the place where he had a spear precisely placed, where it would enter at the right spot. Sometimes spears only injured the whale. This time the whale took the thrust of the spear into the heart; the angle of the canoe and the whale were in perfect position, just as Kee-sta had prayed for. There were times when whalers, in order to capture and kill the whale in shorter time, would jump onto the whale and put a rock into the blowhole. This was not known to have happened to Kee-sta, but other hunters have told stories of how other whales were captured.

That was not the end of the kill. The final act was executed by knife and lance thrust into the area that let all the blood out through the throat of the whale. And the whale, gasping for air, turned over, and when it turned over it was fighting for air because the spear was in the heart and the throat was split open. It was better to keep the lungs inside the whale filled with air, in order for it to float rather than sink. They plugged up the hole inside the throat so that kept even more air in other parts of the whale. Kept afloat this way, the whale could then be towed to shore.

It sometimes took many days to tow the whale from where it was killed to Bartlett Island. Somehow the people in the settlements of Ahousaht and the other parts of Vargas Island and Blunden Island heard of the kill and went out towards where the whale was being towed in, and put a line on it. There were as many as 12 canoes that helped tow the whale in to the beach. I have said the success depended on supernatural assistance and being very well prepared. The hunt was a challenge between man and giant whale, and the whale was both strong and instinctive, aware that it was being hunted by man.

There are names derived from Kee-sta's hunting skill. For instance, the name well known by all was Atlieu, which is the family name passed down to his son Shamrock. Atlieu means "cedar root," and when you twist the cedar root the stringy parts of the root become flexible and like rope. When you make a length of it, you turn the branch, the root, back and forth to make it flexible and not break so that you could join it into many lengths, splice it, and make it into rope.

Kee-sta Atleo, my grandfather, became very wealthy, a famous, successful hunter and title holder to Bartlett Island, his place of preparing for the hunt of the giant whale. My cousin, Gertrude, goes to this island annually to talk to the Creator and to remember the success of our grandfather, a famous hunter, well known from the Queen Charlotte Islands to the Oregon coast. And his success also came from all his years in hunting for other mammals such as the fur seal. The name Chaquosoikmik was bestowed on Kee-sta by the chiefs of the Nuu-Chah-Nulth who attended the ceremony.

The choice parts of the whale were called *chaquosoi*. So the hunter of that whale is called Chaquosoimik, "the one that catches the whale." That was the name of Kee-sta after he captured that whale. Most recently the name belonged to Mark Atleo.

The stories about hunting, whaling, and ambition connect my generation with Kee-sta's; this all ties in with the life of Kee-sta, of Mark Atleo, and of me. We never hunted whale, Mark

Atleo and myself, but we hunted for fur seal. We tried with a spear but we never had success, so we used a shotgun. Because of the law-makers, we were not allowed to shoot fur seal with the shotgun. We were only allowed to use aboriginal tools such as canoe and spear, part of what is called "aboriginal rights and title."

Ktlunoos, Seals in Nuu-Chah-Nulth Life and Culture

Fur seals, called *kwakwatl'* in my language, were and are an important element of the Nuu-Chah-Nulth people's lives. Our part of the coastline is only one part of the wider range of the northern fur seal, because its migration begins as far north as the Pribilof Islands in the Bering Sea. In our area the seals may be found from Dixon Entrance, and the whole coastline of the Haida lands of the Queen Charlottes, to Vancouver Island and as far south as the Gulf of Mexico on the southern parts of their migration.

The northern fur seal is a fascinating creature. The story of its life since humans first put themselves into the seal's habitat is a story of both flagrant plunder and international wildlife conservation, depending on the true meaning of what we call conservation. Our people, the Nuu-Chah-Nulth, knew the times of the seal herds passing, along the coast on their way to the south, stopping to feed on the banks off the coastal waters of Clayoquot Sound and Nootka Sound. The seal herds were fast moving, spending seven months travelling, swimming, and following the fish. They went to the shallow banks and were able to dive and feed on the cod, herring, and salmon to give them strength to swim their long migration.

Before the fur seal became a focus for the European fur industry, it was an important source of food for the coastal people. Our people used the meat and made robes that were very warm and comfortable from their fine fur. Like salmon, whale meat, and whale blubber, the seal meat was smoked for long-term storage. Strips one-quarter inch to a half inch by a foot long were hung above a smoky fire in the sun and wind to preserve the meat for the winter months.

The Europeans who first came among us at Nootka Sound changed our relationship with fur seals. There are two parts to the fur seal hunting story, one that predates the period when fur buyers commercialized the hunt, and another after it became an industry in which many Nuu-Chah-Nulth people participated. There is a cultural and survival difference relating to how and why we hunted fur seal. As a food source, the fur seal is very rich, but the animal is hard to hunt the way our people hunted them, by spear. So our people learned and kept much knowledge about the animals in our culture to aid in our survival.

It is quite an interesting part of life for First Nations people, relying on the seal as a source of food for the many thousands of people that lived along the coastline, especially because we lost our rights to the seals, and younger generations have had little contact with this important animal. Some of the things I will take from my own recollection from boat tanners from Clayoquot Sound and my father-in-law, Keitlah, who was hired on as a hunter when he was just 16 years old, signing articles on the schooners,

Lady Mine and *Jessie*. These were good-sized schooners, each able to take on 12 hunting canoes. Hunting canoes were dug out quite heavily, 16 to 18 feet long, and approximately 4 to 5 feet wide. They were roomy little canoes that were hoisted onto the schooner anchored out in front of Maaqtusiis.

One of the young hunters who joined ship was George Jacobson, who was the same age as Keitlah. The interesting thing about George Jacobson was that he changed his name while on a sailing schooner that took him to hunt the seal herd. The people had Nuu-Chah-Nulth names that were hard for the English-speaking seamen to pronounce. One of the sailors on board the schooner wanted to give him a name that he understood so he said, "You can use my name." His name was Jacobson. There were others that changed to the English names because they were easier to pronounce and to write into the log book.

There were other young hunters who joined the ship at Ahousaht. There was George Si, Noah Thomas, Thomas Louie, Chief Billy, Chief George, Big William, William Swan, Big Paul, Fred Gillet, Chief Joseph. There were also some ladies who joined ship as cooks, including my mother-in-law, Eliza Johnny. These journeys on a sailing schooner often took nine months at a time. The hunters followed the seal herd as it went southward, beginning from the Pribilof Islands, following the herd migrating along the American shoreline en route to the south. This was quite a story, because they had to understand the geography of where they were. But always having been sea-going people, the Nuu-Chah-Nulth understood direction and travel on the sea and quickly learned about the compass points and how they related to navigation.

The story of the fur seal has much importance. It clearly shows an example of the changes to our people's behaviour after the arrival of Europeans. Before the fur buyer/traders came, our people used the aboriginal style of spear with a barb on the end, to go through the skin and into the body of the seal and when you pulled it back, the barb locked a line into place. It was so strong that it would never break. The end of the spear was tied onto a line that fitted into the end of the wooden spear itself. When the spear went into the skin, the rope held, but the wooden part of the spear withdrew. The seal did not die on the impact, but it fought hard to get away pulling the line taut and dragging the canoe here and there. It sometimes took hours for the hunter to get a chance to club the fur seal on the head to lessen its fighting and bring the animal into the canoe. When we started hunting on the schooners, following the herd, we used the canoes to hunt during the day with the same method until there was enough money to buy guns. The guns would kill the seal more quickly.

This is the route that our forefathers took when they started signing on as hunters, seamen, and as cooks for nine months of the year. In California, they went into San Francisco and went ashore and shopped in the big city for clothing, rum, whiskey, cutlery, teapots, kettles, cooking pots, and other things of value, because the hunters were very well off. Some of the hunters made good money selling their seals to the captain of the ship, who was the agent for the company with the authority to pay off the hunter all through the hunting trip.

Part of the changes to our relationship with the seals came from the change in the methods used in the hunt. The new ways of hunting resulted in the depletion of seals on our coast. It also depleted our supply of hunters, due to their participation in the commercial hunt. Eventually, the diminishing seal populations led to conservation measures in the form of an international treaty. The treaty was between the Americans, Russians, Japanese, and British on behalf of Canada, made without any reference to the needs or roles of the Nuu-Chah-Nulth people.

The next major phase in the chronology of the northern fur seal hunt develops farther north, where the Russians had earlier observed herds of seals swimming northward each spring through the passes of the Aleutian chain, disappearing into the fog and mist of the Bering Sea. In 1783, Pribilof, a navigator in the service of Imperial Russia, joined the search for the breeding grounds outside the Commander Islands. His discovery of St. George Island in 1786 and St. Paul in 1787, within a group of islands which now bears his name, exposed the breeding grounds of the northern fur seal to exploitation by humans.

Overnight, the northern fur seals became the source of seal skins for the entire world. During this period, harvesting was uncontrolled and breeding females were unprotected. In 1834, when it was obvious that fur seals were facing extinction, measures were taken and the fur seal populations had begun to recover by 1867 when the United States purchased Alaska from Russia. During the first two years of U.S. jurisdiction, a number of independent seal companies were allowed to operate on the islands. In the first season 200,000 to 300,000 skins were taken, a number now considered to be excessive for the management of the herd.

In 1869, the American Congress established a special reserve to protect the seals' breeding grounds and to provide for controlled harvest. The American government was authorized to award the first of two consecutive 20-year leases for sealing on the island by private companies who took only a specified number of young males. Under the first 20-year lease, the lessee was authorized to take 100,000 young males each year, totalling just under two million seals. One other company was awarded the second lease to take 342,651 seals, probably because the contract period coincided with the peak of pelagic sealing. This unregulated pelagic operation, taking mostly females, was responsible for reducing the l remnant of its former size. Pelagic sealing, primarily b from the United States, Canada, and Japan, reached a 1894, when 610,830 seals were taken. So many animals per year were taken and many more were lost after being wounded. The herd had now been reduced from an estimated two million to probably under 300,000 seals.*

Pelagic sealing was halted in July 1911 as part of an international agreement by the United States, Great Britain (for Canada), Japan, and Russia meeting in Washington. In exchange for the right to pelagic sealing, the United States and Russia agreed to provide Japan and Great Britain each with 15 percent of their seal harvest from the island rookeries. Japan in turn agreed to give the United States, Great Britain, and Russia each 10 percent of its annual harvest of seals on Ramen Island. Thus, in 1911 the agreement became the instrument that finally gave much needed protection to the seal herds, providing economic gain for the countries involved. It was the first significant step towards a type of international cooperation required for the survival of the fur seal.

---

*Editor's note: For details of fur seal populations and takes, see annual NOAA Technical Memoranda, Fur Seal Investigations, National Marine Mammal Laboratory, National Marine Fisheries Service, USDC, Seattle, Washington, 1990, 1992 et al.

The survival of aboriginal people did not seem to receive the same attention. Not only did we lose the employment opportunity, but we lost the right to hunt seals for food except when using traditional hunting methods. I have said a little bit about the importance of the transition from spear to the gun. The double-barrelled 10 gauge or 12 gauge shotguns were very much in demand by the hunters, to get away from having to hold onto a line that burnt your hand and the seal biting the canoe, biting the line, and everything else within its reach in order to save its life. We were told that if we wanted to continue to hunt seal for our own consumption, we would have to return to using a spear.

This area is one in which people have begun to appraise the price they have paid for progress, in the form of a damaged environment and diminished resources. The generations of Nuu-Chah-Nulth people younger than me have no memory of the seal meat and pelts, nor of the precarious journey to offshore waters in small boats. Neither do we have any say in the disposition of the animals that are part of our world, yet are harvested for commercial gain by other peoples. The story of the whale is significant because whales are once again important aspects of the wildlife inhabiting our traditional territory, while the seal provides a good example of the type of changes we have experienced through the transition from first European contact to modern times.

3

The Gift of Salmon

There is a name for "conservation" in the Nuu-Chah-Nulth language: 7uh-mowa-shitl ("keep some and not take all"). This word pertains to careful use of the fishery.

DURING THE EARLY TIMES, the population of the Nuu-Chah-Nulth was about 10,000 or more altogether, so they had to use all the different kinds of salmon resources from all the rivers to catch food fish during the salmon season. There were salmon runs almost every month. The sockeye started to come in May and June. Then came the spring salmon, some in June, July, and August. Then the sockeye came again, in August to September. A heavy run of chum salmon came in October, and lasted right to December.

When we were children, we went along and were shown the Megin River. Somehow the Megin seems to be very important as my heritage from my dad and my grandfather. We spent a lot of time together up the Megin River and into Megin Lake. My dad explained to me that it was like a gift, that came to us, as *Ha'wiih*, the ownership of the land, rivers, and streams. We had a little cabin up at the lake and we had a camp down at the lower end of the river.

It's eight miles from the mouth of the Megin River up to the lake. In the summer, a lot of the stream is quite dry. In some places where the sockeye travel, there are deep pools. The sockeye will stay around those deeper areas until it rains. The fish seem to know that they have to wait for the stream to start flowing over the top of the sandbars and rock and gravel. They have to wait for the rain to come down, to give them a chance to wander up to Megin Lake. Here they find spots to spawn, places where the young eggs will hatch, to survive and then become smolts. When the river is deep enough the young sockeye are able to manoeuvre around, in the deeper places and in the lake. They seem to enjoy their travels along the shorelines and along the upper Megin, eventually to find their way down the river and out into the ocean.

That's the biological wonder. We know very little about how the salmon cycles work. We only see what we see – how the salmon survive to go through the whole routine of finding places to hatch their eggs and then the area that they have to travel around, to grow into a size that will bring them all the way down the river and out to the ocean. They are tiny little fish, yet they go out to the sea, long, long distances, where they move about and grow. By the time they come back to the river and the spawning beds, they are big fish, 12 pounds or so.

HaHuulhi was important to my family and other families that

Chum salmon spawning. HERB HAMMOND

helped look after the fish streams and spawning beds. We used to watch the deep pools going upriver. We spent a lot of time up at the lake, watching the sockeye spawning, and the little salmon hatching out and growing into smolts. From one year to the next, it was alive with the salmon. They went up close to the same time each year, but it was but not always at exactly the same time. Sometimes it was earlier, sometimes later, depending on the weather and the food.

Various other species came up the river too. The cohos came a little later, and the same with the spring salmon. When they came in the fall months of September, October, November, they were a huge size, some of them as heavy as 40 pounds. The chum salmon came in the fall of the year, in October. The survival of all these fish was very important for our people.

A young girl with a hair seal on a wheelbarrow.

My dad liked to hunt. I wasn't shown too much about hunting, but my dad used to hunt and trap, and it was more or less as we needed it, like food on the table. Our hunting started in November, after the fish had dwindled in the rivers, so my dad would like to change our diet to meat. During the years that my dad used to hunt we'd have some deer, *muuwach* meat. For some reason we never shot or killed the black bear. We saw them around, but my dad never bothered to shoot them. It was the *muuwach*, the deer meat, that he looked for. There were a few elk, but none in our area. They lived further inland, more in what they call the Strathcona Park area now. There was other things like fur seal, that were part of our diet. There was also hair seal; my dad used to go hunting for the hair seal close to the rivers, because that's where they were feeding, on salmon that were coming up to spawn.

My dad was a very quiet person, but he taught us how to survive in the woods. He used to knock down great big fir trees on the hill above where our little shack was, to keep our fires going. We had woodstoves, which my dad had bought, and we kept the fire going, for doing our cooking. In his quiet way, our dad taught us what life was about. Also, we had a grandfather who lived to a full life of close to 100 years. He brought us into the woods and showed us a spiritual understanding of the animals and fish and anything else that we used.

As I said, the knowledge of how the salmon moved about in season was very important. The young salmon don't move out of the river until they are about three or four inches long, and then they start to swim in the channels, back and forth. They seem to know when it is time to go out into the open sea, and to know the places where they can go and feed on other things out in the ocean. They seem to follow the warm water areas out in the Pacific Ocean, way up north, following the Japanese Current. After about four years they start looking for directions to return to their own stream. They have knowledge of where they came out, and they go back to their own stream. Then, another cycle is completed.

Nature can be strong and wicked, or fair, depending on the time of the year. Heavy rains in Clayoquot Sound and along the coastline would bring down wood, even giant cedar and spruce logs down the rivers. Sometimes the bottom of the rivers was plugged up with debris 40 or 50 feet high.

Our people knew that a washout could completely damage the salmon eggs that were in the gravel. They had knowledge to look after the debris, there was knowledge also of not completely cleaning out places where logs were jammed. Sometimes they

An old-growth forest and hydro-riparian ecosystem with fallen trees that create important in-stream structures for fish. HERB HAMMOND

couldn't move the big logs, and the big chunks of wood became protection for the salmon and their eggs from the heavy rains in the fall, when the streams rose. The fish could dig down beside the logs in the gravel.

They have been caring for the fish and looking after the streams for years – in the Megin, Cypre, Alteo, Mohenya, Bedwell, Warn Bay. They had makeshift frameworks for cabins, so when they moved back to Ahousaht after the fishing season, in the beginning or middle of November, they loaded the loose boards and towed them to Ahousaht, to fill in the holes in their houses there. These boards were called *lhú7uuk*.

Cleaning the rivers was a duty to the Ahousaht people. There were various ways that people were tied in to stream care. I learned from Paul Sam. I went to the rivers with him and watched how it was done. If there was a big jam, you couldn't move it, but he would dig around it. When the stream lowered and dried out in the summer, the fish found that the best place to lay their eggs was at the far side, underneath a big log. There in the shelter of the log the little fry were safe. People sometimes used to take the eggs in the gravel and move them to a good location, if the stream was jammed up, or if it changed its course. The old people knew the practices. I have never moved the salmon eggs myself, but Paul Sam did this. He even used the male milt to fertilize the eggs that he moved.

My wife Josephine told me that there was a stream in Esperanza Inlet, where she comes from, where the fish weren't coming back. A man went over to the hop yards, along the Fraser River near Chilliwack, and brought home sockeye eggs and milt and planted them in the stream, and the sockeye came back, with the fish from Chilliwack. This stream was named _7aw7alts'e_ ("big river") after the Fraser River, from where the fish came.

There is a name for "conservation" in the Nuu-Chah-Nulth language: _7ub-mowa-shitl_ ("keep some and not take all"). This word pertains to careful use of the fishery. People knew how much they could use, and they didn't ever use it all. They did have big feasts at the beginning and the end of the salmon run to celebrate the gift of the salmon.

There were years when no fish came up the rivers. The word for this is _wikĺns7ii_ ("cycle never arrived"). It wasn't good for the people, and they had to turn to other foods. Mostly, there were shellfish. You'll find under the ground at Ahousaht layers several

Kukuhw'isa – hair seal, an important Nuu-Chah-Nulth food source.
ROBERT D. TURNER

feet deep of clam shells, mussel shells. It took a lot to feed 10,000 people.

The people looked after all the resources they depended on. They also hunted ducks, and deer that came in, and the hair seal and the fur seal. So, there was dependence on other resources besides salmon. There were times when the people got pretty lean. There were edible plants too. For example, there was some kind of a root they used in really bad times; it was a sugar root, a source of sugar.

4

Plants as Food and Medicine

*The islands near the ocean are very special and
sacred places....Here you can get close to the
Creator and to many medicinal plants.*

Fish and other meats were only a part of our support from nature.
Plants too played a large role. I remember going by canoe to the
smaller outlying islands near Flores Island. The plants were
different on these islands, facing the Pacific Ocean. One plant,
called *chashxiwa7* (thimbleberry shoots), grew in rocky areas along
the shoreline. It was not an evergreen. It grew about three feet tall,
and was a little thicker than a pencil. It was like a briar. You broke
off the stem at the bottom, peeled off the skin. It is bright green,
watery and very clean, with no prickles, and it is very tasty. The
kids used to bring a little sugar along, and dip the end in sugar

Thimbleberry: both the berries and the young, peeled shoots (*chashxiwa7*) are good to eat. NANCY J. TURNER

before they ate it. These shoots only grow in the month of June, or early July. During the season the plant hardens when it becomes part of the branch and then is too woody to eat.

The ladies around Ahousaht used to bring in armfuls of *chashxiwa7* from the outer islands and called the other women to come and help with it. The kids used to eat it, and they'd give them a little bit. Men ate some, but very little; it was a belief that this food was for women. They had it with "cheese" made out of fish eggs, which was dried and smoked in the smoke house.

Another plant similar to *chashxiwa7* is *q'ilhtsup* (cow parsnip, or wild celery). It grows in the same area, on the outer islands, close to the thimbleberry. It was picked separately, not mixed with *chashxiwa7*. The *q'ilhtsup* is a plant enjoyed by both men and women, but it is available for a shorter time period. It hardens much more quickly; you can only get it for a short time, usually in June. By July, it's hardened noticeably. It has a distinctive colour, reddish, mixed with a greenish colour on the part you peel off; the red is sort of the colour of rhubarb. It has no prickles, but you always have to peel it before you eat it.

Another plant the Nuu-Chah-Nulth people liked in spring, which is also very filling, is called *ma7yi* (salmonberry shoots). People used it as a travelling food. It is very juicy. Most young people picked its new growth when it first came out; they gathered it by the armload and shared it with men, women, and children. Things have changed; they don't do that now. Today, things are not practised the way they used to be, when people gathered. Now the people eat rhubarb, lettuce, cabbage, carrots, peas. Very few people go to the bush, although Jo and I go and have a feed when we can. We really enjoy it. We used to go to the islands in the early part of June, before the seagull eggs become ripe, at the first laying of the seagull eggs. Then we'd have a feed of seagull eggs, and we'd also have some *q'ilhtsup*. The island we went to often is called qutumkH (Cleland Island, or, as the fishermen call it, Bear Island). It's got every type of plant you would want to see in early growth (May and June) including plants that don't grow on Flores Island.

The islands near the ocean are very special and sacred places. They give privacy and a place for spiritual retreat. A person can wash himself clean in the pools along the shore that are replenished by the rain. There are big basins of water, and little gravelly or sandy beaches for swimming. Here you can get close to the Creator and to many medicinal plants. There is secrecy surrounding the medicinal plants. There is one particular kind, called *mulhmuts,* which grows only at one season of the year on those islands. The Creator put it there for only a very short period of time, to be used in one's spiritual life. You can tell this plant because of its sweetness, and because it is only there for a short time. It is used for building up and cleansing the body. It refreshes the system of life inside and out. If you are afflicted with some things you can't heal, it has the power to cleanse part of your body. It has an antibiotic; it cleans out your kidneys, your liver and your lungs. Indian doctors or other spiritual people made a potion, or preserve of this medicine, in the form of a paste. They kept this salve in a container made out of alder wood. The container

Cow parsnip, or wild celery (*q'ilhtsup*); young shoots are edible when peeled.
NANCY J. TURNER

was made by hollowing out a section of trunk from a young alder tree at the first stages of growth. It carves easily when it is green; then it is hardened and fitted with a lid. It is about four or five inches high and three inches across. The container kept this special root medicine moist, so it wouldn't dry out.

People came from far away and paid a high price to see and receive treatment from the Indian doctors. The price was not in

Salal berries, called *yam'a7*, a favourite food. NANCY J. TURNER

money, but in skins and furs of bear, raccoon, mink, and otter, all highly valued. Sometimes the Indian doctors traded some of their medicine; they put a tiny bit in a smaller flask. This medicine would give stronger protection from evil sources, to ward off bad wishes and thoughts from those wishing harm to a person. I met some of these Indian doctors, spiritual leaders, when I was young.

Many of our medicines are sacred. They are used in different ways. For example, *tuHmapt,* young spruce, is used to scare off evil spirits, and *qwitl'aqmapt,* hemlock, is used for cleansing the body, as a scrubber, and for spiritual purposes. Cascara bark is used as a laxative (and is called *shutsiqmpat,* "laxative"). Back in the 1930s and 1940s, commercial buyers came in and bought dried cascara bark, and they kind of made it scarce in the Clayoquot area. Now you have to go deep in the woods or up the lakes and rivers to find it.

Yew is called *tl'atmapt*. Healers would make juice from the bark and use it as a medicine for ailing people who had no hope and were almost on their deathbeds. They took the bark off and placed the inner part into some warm water and soaked it, so that the sap would meet the water. It was this juice they used for drinking. It was a very successful medicine. A lot of yew bark is being used by people in the medical field now.

Ferns and some other greenery, called *tla7qa7pt*, are used for open sores that can't be healed, and for boils and infections. You cover the infected skin with the leaves as a poultice, and they draw out the infection. Stinging nettle, called *ilhmapt*, was used for medicine too. They took the sticky part of the snail, the slime, and ground it together with nettles. Then they used this mixture for spiritual protection to keep away evil.

After the Europeans came, the numbers of Nuu-Chah-Nulth, once around 10,000 strong, were drastically reduced. Sometimes our people were struck with diseases that had no medicine good enough or strong enough to revive them. These were bad sicknesses, like the ones called "flu" in today's terms. In one bad year of influenza or some other type of sickness that had no medication, the 10,000 went down very quickly to 5,000. Then the numbers went to 2,000 and hung around there for a long time. Now the numbers are slowly coming back.

Ladies in the villages first picked plant foods in the spring time, *tl'aqshilh*. The summer, called *tl'upichH*, was the time for picking berries, such as salal, called *yam'a7*. Jo loves to pick these berries. I worked for the Coast Guard for 30 years, and we used to go to the Coast Guard base at Hope Island, where Jo picked gallons and gallons of *yam'a7*, and made them into jam. You can also preserve the berries by drying them in the sun; the dried berries look like raisins. You can also hang them up, while they are still attached to their stems and branches, or lay them out on a mat. Either way, you can keep them through the winter. The people used to roll them into mats, or place them in openwork baskets of cedar bark, so that the air could circulate around them.

People often stored berries and smoked fish in very large baskets or containers, called *tla7pa7t*. These are like a big box, with cedarwood corners. There are no nails. The bottom and sides are made with a basket weaving of spruce root woven in and out. The bottom, sides, and lid are all made out of spruce roots. These roots grow very long, from very young spruce trees. A young Sitka spruce, just a couple of feet high, is called *tuHmapt*.

There is another coastal berry, found near the ocean. It is called *qawi* (salmonberry). It's the same plant that gives you *ma7yi*. The flower blooms in May, and the berries come in June. It is pinkish, and the berries are yellow or red, and very delicious. They look much like raspberries. When there are a lot of salmonberries out, there's going to be a lot of sockeye. The Nuu-Chah-Nulth people know this. The bushes grow along rivers and streams. There are some right around Ahousaht, and some at Moyena, at Herbert Inlet. There are two rivers there, and people would come back from there with buckets of *qawi*. The salmon coming back to the river will be equal to the numbers of berries found on the bushes.

Wild cranberries (bog cranberries), called *pa7pa7is*, are found in swamps and bogs. In order to find them, the people had to go through the bush and into the swampland around Flores Island. These berries were usually quite scarce. Even today, *pa7pa7is* is very hard to find. It is different from the cultivated cranberries. It

Salmonberry: the berries range in colour from golden to dark red; the shoots, called *ma7yi*, are peeled and eaten in spring. NANCY J. TURNER

grows very low, right on the marsh, in the moss. In Ahousaht, it grew in the swampland between the outer beaches and the inner harbour. Quite a few of the commercial cranberries were brought in by the missionaries and planted in the field by the residential school. There used to be a lake where this field is today. It was a sockeye producing lake, called *a7uqnak* ("a place with a lake"), which was also the name of the residential school. When the missionaries came, they had the schoolboys, even the very little boys, dig a long ditch, and they drained the lake and brought in the commercial cranberries. Then somebody else bought the property, and they uprooted some of the cranberries with an earth digger and they started planting nursery-type plants there. I've seen a lot of destruction, destruction to the forest and to the land. Across the water from my home, there are bald hills there now, where there used to be nothing but forests.

There are two other berries, different from each other, but with the same look. One is *tsisma7pt*; it is a vine, with tiny berries. When you press the berries, it looks like blood. The berries are found way up in the mountains, at high altitude. It survives there in the cold, in later months, September and October. This is blackcap. The other berry is called *His-shitl* ("bleed"), which is prickly and has small, tiny leaves that look like a blackberry. It is very thin; it grows in long, long strings, 20 to 30 feet long. It is found along the highway between Port Alberni and Ucluelet, and in the Nahmint Valley. This is the trailing blackberry. It seems since logging has cleared away trees up in the hills, the berries grow more, until the new trees crowd them out. The Port Alberni ladies go out specially for these berries. They get lots in July and August, but the berries are so tiny.

Another kind of berry is *qa7lhkinta7piH*, wild (seaside) strawberries. These are tiny little strawberries that grow on the open hillsides. There are some around Ahousaht, and around the residential school, on the rocks. They cling to the sparse moss that grows in crevices on the rocks. You don't find them high up, and there are not enough to make jam with. Instead, you eat them on the spot.

Another wild berry is called *milhka7um*. This is a small, greenish berry on a bush about three feet high, and the berries grow in clusters. These are wild black gooseberries. There are some kinds that are grown by farmers that are fairly big. You can make jam from them. Some of the wild ones become reddish and then very dark. They are the size of a small raisin, some even smaller, and very sour.

Wild crabapple is called *tsitsiHa7qtlmapt*. It was an important

Pacific yew — *tl'atmapt*; an important tough wood, and also a medicine; source of anti-cancer drug taxol. NANCY J. TURNER

food in the old days. Bunchberry is another one. It has bright red berries growing in little clusters, and is called *hastachi*. Another berry is called *situp*. It is a little blueberry that grows in June and July, and is very sweet. It looks the same as a store-bought blueberry. It is not a berry that has heavy growth, though; it is slight and small. You can find it in the inner bush, where you find salal. Red huckleberry is called *hisinwa*. It grows in summer. Another berry is *sinumxits*. It is a fall berry that looks like red huckleberry, but starts to ripen in September and October. The berries grow in clusters and are small, firm, and very dark.

Right from the beginning of the year to the end, people were never idle around Ahousaht. There are beautiful beaches, beautiful lands; you never worried about food. This is the life my father and my mother lived after finishing grade eight and being discharged from the residential school to go and learn how to catch fish, smoke fish, and go from place to place, wherever the salmon was running in the 24 streams of Clayoquot Sound.

5

ʼNaaʼsQaʔitkquisHicit:
Our Changing Landscape

*These are the foundation and the context of my
thoughts on the state of First Nations people in British
Columbia and where the future might take us.*

*I*N THIS CHAPTER I WILL PRESENT some of the memories of myself
and my people. Together, these are the foundation and the context
of my thoughts on the state of First Nations people in British
Columbia and where the future might take us. It is important for
the reader to realize that some things that are taken for granted
by white people are quite different from how a First Nations
person might think. I discuss some of the spiritual beliefs we
have and their links to the land and waters that surround us. I

write here about our version of the origins of the Nuu-Chah-Nulth in Clayoquot Sound. Many older people that surrounded me during my life have given me their perspectives, mainly through stories and songs. I will present some of those and explain what they mean to us.

I want to talk about my village and the life I led in and around the village and the people of Ahousaht. The period of my parents' and my life is one of great change. As the white society developed, we joined the labour force of some industries but were widely excluded from many economic activities. Some of those very activities, like logging and commercial fishing, both of which I have taken part in, came to reduce much of the resource base that had supported us throughout our lives on Vancouver Island.

Naa's Qa?itkquisHicit

Naa'sQa?itkquisHicit is a Nuu-Chah-Nulth word meaning the changing ways of Mother Earth and all the surrounding elements, from every avenue of life. It refers to the cycles, the water coming from the mountainsides in spring and the stream gushing out of the rocky hillside, running down into the ocean, and from the ocean evaporating back up into the skies to transform once again into rainwater.

It refers to the change in summer when the sun dries out the hillsides, the riverbanks, and the ocean shores. Living things, including humans, rely on the summer season for food, be it fish, deer, seal, berries, or all the resources of the ocean. All rely on the changing ways of Mother Nature according to the time of year.

In the fall, when the huge leaves start falling off the maple trees, the summer's growth goes back into the ground. With the fall comes the changing colours of a beautiful hillside. Then comes the wintry weather, where we get a bit of cold, snow, and ice.

We see smolts coming from the rivers; fish of different species have different seasons to return to the ocean. All this is also dependent on time. Within the lives of human beings and animals, we only see a very small part of this great change and the way it happens. What I have seen in my lifetime, 76 years of being one of the living creatures, leaves me very much unsure of how we now relate to cycles of the year and the longer time elements of animals and their environment.

Spring, summer, fall, and winter all have Nuu-Chah-Nulth names. Early spring we call *tl'aqshi*, which means "growth." *Tl'op'ichH* means "warm summer weather," and *ʔay'ichH* means "fall season." *Ts'oʔichH* refers to the wash-down of all mountainsides, all rivers, cleaned out by torrents of water coming from the winter.

The four directions of wind also have names. In the summer we have westerly winds, called *huchclitch*. Southeasterly stormy winds are called *tuchilth*. The cold north wind that brings arctic air is called *yuhtacak*.

Tiskin

During the stormy weather it is easy to remember how we are kept in contact with the Tiskin, the almighty Thunderbird. The

Thunderbird is the main element that links our lives to the seasons and the weather. It is the heart of our interconnectedness. The lightning is *kli-cliba* and Tiskin is the thunder, made by the giant Thunderbird.

It is important to know how we look into the sky towards the west and then towards the southeast, to understand what the weather is going to be like. The elders would look into the sky and say, "Tiskin, how is the weather going to be today?" And Tiskin would answer, "I'll give you rain. I'll give you wind. All for the sake of the living creatures, whatever it may be, animals, human beings, or fish in the ocean." We could understand the conditions and were seldom wrong because Tiskin showed what the day would be like, what the week would be like, or what the month would be like. The moon and the sun were very important parts of understanding Mother Nature, Tiskin, and human beings and animals and life on Planet Earth. That is how we understand the elements of the universe.

Every knowledgeable person in the Nuu-Chah-Nulth Nation understands what I have written here about Tiskin and the weather and seasons. Knowing our environment on a day-to-day basis was important in order to have a safe journey. If, in the past, for example, you were travelling 30 to 50 miles out into the ocean hunting fur seal and whale (things I discuss in other parts of this book), knowing the weather conditions was important for survival. You could decide not to go out due to bad weather, based on the knowledge of elders who would sing during the stormy weather. They would sing to Tiskin, to ask him to please calm our waters in dangerous times of the year when people were travelling on the coast, be it going for feasts or visits to other tribes along the coast.

Tiskin was here before life was formed. He was here before the creation of humankind. Tiskin is sacred; he holds the world in his wings. We are not fooled because he is not visible, for we know his spirit is in all areas that are moving on the face of the earth: the weather and the seasons.

The song of the Thunderbird is what gives us success, like that we had in our battles with the Otsosat Nation that I discussed earlier in this book. Tiskin was there on our side. We learned from Tiskin the value of being a strong person, gaining strength from the abundant foods that we ate. If we dug up the sand on aboriginal land, we would find a wealth of shellfish, which was what Tiskin also ate.

It is known, though, that a true believer can talk to Tiskin. He becomes angry, mostly when he sees examples of selfishness. He is happy when everyone is included in the feast of the giant whale or other animals of the sea. Lately, during treaty talks in Nootka that I will also discuss later, the Ahousaht brought seal blubber and meat and home-baked bannock to the table. The table was loaded with food. I wonder if my nation knew that Tiskin joined the feast by spirit and was happy to watch nations at peace?

The gifts of Tiskin are like instinct. I talk to Tiskin, he talks to me, and I hear, but it is not like you hear other things. It is more of an understanding of what is right and what is wrong. Simple ways of life; harmony with nature and Tiskin. I believe that Tiskin would be very pleased that I am mentioning him in my work here. My hopes and my dreams are to meet Tiskin in person, to tell him what I have put on paper and why I have done so. He will be happy to know that we very much respect his strength, his presence, and his spirit in body and soul. I say "soul" more for the English version of the spirit Tiskin and my spirit.

The Beginnings of Our Nations

The story I am presenting here came to me from the late Francis Charlie. He was the younger brother of Chester Charlie, the hereditary chief of the Keltsomaht and a self-taught historian with special knowledge of the history of the amalgamation of the Ahousaht First Nation. His story is about the early movement and arrival of the First Nations into Clayoquot Sound. It was when our nations were formed, on the advice of Tiskin.

Some time ago there was a freeze-up of the inlets, mountains, waterways, channels, and the rivers all through Clayoquot Sound, from the areas of Bear River, the inlets in and around Meares Island, Warn Bay, and through the outside areas, both sides of Fortune Channel and the Cypre River. The whole of Bedwell Sound was frozen over, and the ice and heavy snow forced people to abandon Bedwell River, Cypre River, Fortune River, Warn Bay, and the villages throughout Catface Mountain, called *Chetapi* in our language, in between Maaqtusiis and Vargas Island.

Francis Charlie's story is kept only by word of mouth, an oral history passed on from generation to generation as to our origin. His story is of all the nations joining together, not finding any enemies, but friends, becoming a nation, understanding the need for survival during that freeze-up and ice that formed throughout Clayoquot Sound. Francis Charlie said there was so much cold that people froze to death because there was no way of freeing wood to make fires. People sought the best places to go for a little bit of warmth. They joined together and found people who maintained driftwood fires on the outer west side of the islands — Flores, Bartlett, Blunden, and Vargas, with its long beach. Some arrivals to the outer beaches were strangers, some were relatives, and some were friends.

If I were to guess as to the time, I would suspect that it would be as long ago as 4,000 years or more. This comes from the archaeological sites near Hesquiat that have indicated human presence over 4,000 years ago. We believe that we did not come from the north across the Bering Strait. There's nothing in our history that I recollect that talks about migration of the Nuu-Chah-Nulth Nation. Rather, our history tells about the movement to get away from the freeze-up of the waters in Clayoquot Sound.

Around that time, there was a plague that engulfed all the nations on the west Pacific coastline all the way to Alaska and all the way to Mexico and the American coastline.

Tiskin appeared and faced the Nuu-Chah-Nulth nations and said, "Form your nations, and I will help in cleaning off the bad omens of disease and plague, and enrich the islands and the coastline from one end to the other on the Pacific shoreline." This may sound like a fairy tale, but the nations were formed on the advice of Tiskin, and we became a spiritually and physically enriched people.

Much of our culture was also created by Tiskin. The song of Tiskin has remained in the minds of our singers. Some songs are for occasions such as feasts or happy times, when people just wanted to enjoy a song and dance for entertainment. Other songs that came out were songs for inspiration. Some songs are ancient, and some are new.

Some songs were for gatherings when First Nations from the many tribes put on a sacred celebration. Tiskin would use his powers to help when the ceremony was on, using other animals such as wolves and bears in the process. There is a sacred gathering under Tiskin's guidance when there is a wish to clear the air of many wrongdoings such as warfare or some bad times that came about from human error. Tiskin would help to give people happy times.

Many types of strong feelings exist, and there are gifted people who can use magic. There are sorcerers, witches, devils, and other such figures, such as those that exist among people around the world. The power of evil exists, and the power of good exists. There are happy times and sad times: sad times when many people die within a short time of each other. When a person dies young, be it suicide or be it from accident, a cycle of life is in play, and we record or remember the death of young people and the sadness that comes with it when a person does not live a full life.

White people that first wanted to teach First Nations modern religious beliefs (I say "modern" because it is a different way of life which does not agree with First Nations) told us something totally different from the culture of First Nations. We understand the different styles, ways, words, and beliefs of non-First Nations. We are open to other beliefs, because we knew something about differences from those within our own Nations. However, I think that the day is quickly passing when we are convinced that we can live two lives with different ways, styles, and beliefs. We all go by inspiration of song, of dance, of praying to Tiskin. We are trying to convince the non-First Nations of the province of British

Columbia and the country of Canada that we are able to control our own destiny. Part of controlling our own way in the world has to do with what white people call resources. We have had some history with resources.

Recollections of Fish and Forests

The purpose of this part of the book is to understand the ideas of resources and how they are linked to working in the white way. The information I use is based mainly on my personal recollections of the role fishing played in my family history, and forestry in my own personal history. This is part of a dialogue I have assembled from speaking with many Nuu-Chah-Nulth elders: Francis Charlie, my grandfather Peter Webster, John Thomas of the Ditidaht, James Adams, Fred Gillette, and F. Mistak. These people, and others, formed a group whose collective knowledge was passed on to me in various forms at different times. I cannot sort some of these early memories out and attribute them to specific individuals. I present them here as a combination of stories from specific people, and as a general understanding I derived from the people who surrounded me.

I have photographs of and memories of Mistak in his younger days, a happy, smiling and healthy man. A really grown person, in the giant sense, a healthy person. He was a genuine Nuu-Chah-Nulth elder who practised sleight of hand and magic for us when we were children. He used to put a coin in his hand, turn his hand over, and the coin would disappear. And playing with cards, he would put down a bunch of cards, lay them all face down, and he would ask us all to take one each and then tell us what we had in our hand before we turned it up.

My grandfather Peter Webster, who passed away a few years ago, remembered beautiful songs. Some of his songs he learned from his father, passed down from past generations. These songs were about happiness, life, survival, and the movement of nations with other nations. The happiness songs were also about the celebration of the resources that came very mysteriously from the ocean. Without too much chasing or trying to do things the hard way, the First Nations sat at the stream waiting for the fish to come up the river. The songs are still being sung today.

Peter Webster told me about the environment, about our knowledge of the cycle of life. He maintained that the people knew how to look after resources and managed to keep the salmon coming up the same stream each year. The mystery for us was, how did these little fish know what to do when they hatched, and how did they know when they were ready to travel down the river out into the ocean, swimming the many miles of coastline following the current, and then return back at various times to the same streams on a cycle? Sometimes it happened that fish did not come back abundantly. But whatever the wrong was, it happened out at sea.

Peter Webster told me another story about the people of Ahousaht who went way up into the mountains looking for a very important resource. He was using the story to present the importance of good cedar for dugout canoes. There are different kinds of canoes for different tasks. They went to locate a place where people could find bigger and better cedar that was not cross-grained, or trees that grew rather in a knot, circle-ish and short, a round tree. They eventually found the trees with the best grain and softness for the best dugout canoes.

The dugout canoe has been around for thousands of years. I would like to bring that time back again, when the first dugout was pulled out of the woods by 20 men. The method for building a canoe was to burn the side of the log and dig the burned parts off the inner side of the dugout canoe. We built huge canoes this way; some were 50 feet long and five or six feet wide at the widest part of the canoe, then tapering off on each end. This was Peter Webster's story of the cedar.

There was no quarrel as to who had the ownership of resources. The people of the Nuu-Chah-Nulth Nation were the stewards, the caretakers, the people that watched the resource. Part of that watching meant keeping in mind the entire watersheds, which has only recently become part of the thinking of government resource managers.

Francis Charlie told me that where they lived, on the south side of Vargas Island, there were no big rivers. There was a little stream on the west end of the island where a few coho salmon came in to spawn. The people depended on the other places that had abundant fish. When they heard there was a run of fish going into the bigger rivers, they were allowed to go there, because the people shared to meet the needs of other tribes that had no streams. So, although Francis Charlie always maintained that they owned no streams, it was not entirely true because the sharing of all the resource was very much a part of the culture of the Nuu-Chah-Nulth Nation.

During the early part of my life in the 1930s and early 1940s, I recall in the early summers the people were home in Ahousaht, and June saw the beginning of the calm and beautiful early summer days. The summer holidays usually started on June 18 or 19, when the children used to go home from the residential schools to their parents for the summer months. Around that week the adults usually started to move towards the fish canneries located up and down the coast. The Ahousaht usually went up to the Rivers Inlet area called Oweekeno, where there were fish canneries. One year I went up with my parents, and my aunt and uncle, to work in a fish cannery during the heavy sockeye run. I have never seen so many sockeye at one time.

Work in the canneries was strenuous. The workday started around eight o'clock in the morning, when the cannery workers, strong women, started filling the cans full of fish — sockeye — cut by machines and cleaned by men and women. There were Chinese workers, too, as many as 40 or 50 of them in each cannery. These people held key jobs, rolling the cans from the storage areas in the upper part of the cannery. The Chinese went around the tables, and when a tray was filled with canned fish they collected it and punched a number on a ticket showing each tray that the worker had filled. The people were experts at estimating the right amount of fish, not too much, so that the lid of the can would fit snugly, covering the fish. The Chinese workers then soldered a lid onto the can, a lengthy operation.

If you were to take a trip over the waters of Oweekeno, there were miles and miles of waterways where the fish were heading to spawn. But there were also well over a thousand gillnetters with their nets strung out in the water and hauling in the gillnets early in the morning. The majority of the boats were wooden skiffs, with one or two people running the net. The fishermen were from all over the coast, from Vancouver, the interior of Vancouver Island, Sechelt, Campbell River, Powell River, Alert Bay, the areas of the Johnstone Strait, and many of the villages on the west coast of Vancouver Island, waking up each morning to work in the fish canneries.

Back in Ahousaht, the summer months became very lonely because all that was left in the village site of Maaqtusiis were the elders, who were unable to work in the fish canneries. There were very few of us left; I was one of those when I was young because I didn't have any place to go at times. There were times that I stayed right at the residential school for the summer months.

The preparation to go north took several weeks of collecting enough food to eat on the way up and to have for living at various canneries. At that time we had small boats, about 30 feet long, powered by engines that we called "one-lungers." We quickly learned how to operate the early boat motors that were introduced to our people. There were motors built by the Easthope Brothers in Steveston, British Columbia, on the south arm of the Fraser River, and Vivian engines manufactured in Vancouver. They were reliable motors, with heavy flywheels and small coiled batteries to fire up the spark plugs. I was shown how to operate small engines when I was growing up.

That long journey would take three to four days of travelling, stopping on the first day perhaps as far from Ahousaht as Kyuquot Sound. Usually in the late evening there would be as many as 30 to 40 boats, each 25 to 30 feet long, anchoring out with the people resting overnight at Kyuquot.

The journey to the Rivers Inlet fish canneries could be very dangerous for the small boats travelling up the coast. The travellers put a canvas cover over from the cabin to the stern of the boat for the trips. That is where the ladies and children had protection from the cold and rain. The environment was always an uncertainty, but our people were familiar with the anchorages up and down the coast that they would use for shelter. Although beautiful in the summer, the sea can be treacherous with its winds and tidal streams. When the tides are strong they rise up to 12 or 13 feet, and the current runs offshore along the outer side of places like Estevan Point at the tip of the Hesquiat Peninsula. Those conditions can be perilous for a small boat taking water into the hold with the weight of the passengers, as many as 20 in the family, and often several families. Thinking of these boat trips up the coast to the canneries reminds me of my very first experience as a worker there, when I was still a boy.

My $13.00 Summer

As I was growing up, spending my time at the residential school next to the Ahousaht Reserve, as it is called by government officials who ran the place for First Nations children to learn the English language, my thoughts and dreams carried me out into the waters and lands far beyond the school. I'll leave the residential school behind, though, just for a beginning of this short story. My dream was always looking out from the school at the passageway between Flores Island, Vancouver Island across the way, for about a mile across Millar Channel. The time I will be telling about is when I was 12 years old. I used to get a very lonely feeling, being one of the students attending this residential school.

We had a beachfront, a sandy beach. Some days I'd be alone down on that beach when the tide was out, and I'd play with the homemade boats that I had carved out of cedar, very rough handiwork, using a scout knife. I used to sit there in the sand and put my boat on the sand, pretending the beach was the channel. There were odd times that there would be a powerboat going by, puttering along, either passing or coming into the channel, as I looked out from the beach. All the other children were away; they had left the school for the summer to go with their parents up to the fish canneries in Rivers Inlet.

My father had a little boat call *The Native Lass*. It was made of cedar, was about 30 feet long, a combination gillnet-troller, powered by a single-cylinder, a "one-lunger." The year when I was 12, I had seen my dad repairing the one-lunger. He had stripped the engine, a Fairbanks, right from top to bottom and had fixed all its moving parts. The engine had a fair-sized flywheel, maybe about 2 feet across. It was bolted onto a crankshaft that fitted onto the bottom part, which was heavy steel plate. This simple boat would take us all the way up to the central coast.

The gas engine which my father had repaired right on the dock where the boat was tied up was only one part of the repair. He had to also finish repairing the boat, putting in new planking, a keel, some decking, and the cabin. It made a very nice-looking boat, made by the expert boatbuilder my father had become by repairing boats all his life.

My dad's promise to me was that I'd be on the boat to Rivers Inlet in the month of June to find my way to places that I'd never been before. I'd never gone anywhere, except just on the ordinary trails through to the village and to the outside beaches.

My dad finished the engine overhaul, and the middle of June came pretty fast, when we were all released from the residential school for the summer. So, we went, stopping in places like Hotspring Cove in Clayoquot Sound, Friendly Cove, Nootka Sound – various other villages. We anchored out in places like Nuchatlitz, Queen's Cove, and in the mornings we left early. At last, I was starting to have a happy summer, because I'd never been outside of the residential school. In my 12th year I was to learn to gill-net in my dad's boat.

We stopped here and there, all along the coastline of Vancouver Island. I mustn't forget to mention that we had a boatload of people who were going up with us to work in the cannery. There were at least 12 people, as I had come along, and my dad had put a tarpaulin over the back end of the boat where the ladies and the young people were sitting or sleeping. My dad was doing a favour to these people that had come along on the boat to find work in the fish canneries.

We went into Rivers Inlet after travelling around Cape Scott on the northern tip of Vancouver Island, and then across the way to Rivers Inlet to the place called Good Hope Cannery. The fishery was going to start on the Sunday night. There was a gun that went off when the season was officially opened, so you could put your net in the water and start the fishing. We reached Rivers Inlet with 300 or 400 other boats that were going fishing like we were. A lot of them had men and women and children who were going to work in the fish cannery. My dad said, "You should apply for work. You might make a few dollars in the fish cannery," and I

Interior of gut-shed Mctavish Cannery, Rivers Inlet. COURTESY OF BC
ARCHIVES COLLECTIONS G03513

agreed. So we went to see the Chinese boss, who was taking in the
applications of those who wanted to work in the fish cannery.
His office was in the China House in the inner part of the cannery.
The cannery itself was built on pilings and decking that went out
over the water.

So I got hired on as an ordinary labourer in the cannery. The
work started at eight o'clock in the morning. I questioned the
boss as to how much my work was going to bring me: what were
they going to pay me? The boss said, "We start you off at 15 cents
an hour, which is not very much, but that's the pay the Chinese
labourer gets, and that's the pay you also will be getting." So, that
was the beginning of my summer holidays. My dad was out fishing
with my younger brother, out on *The Native Lass*, out towards the
open ocean. I was in the cannery.

There were other young people who were hired on in the

cannery, but many quit as soon as they saw what kind of work they had to do, and also how much pay they would be getting. I thought about quitting on the first day too. It seemed like a very long day, 17 hours on the first day of my job in the fish cannery. It was very demanding work. I had to sit at the end of a chute, just big enough for the cans to roll down from the upper part of the second storey of the building, where Chinese workers were rolling the cans down. I waited until the basket that held the cans was full and then quickly pulled the filled basket away and put an empty one in its place. The baskets full of cans were brought to the ladies who were packing the cans. And when each can was filled, the lady put it on a conveyor belt and all the cans moved along the line of the conveyor belt, held in a tray for them to go through the steamer.

The salmon was steamed to get rid of the blood that might be on the fish. There were many things wrong with the fish. Although it was fresh when it arrived, it took only one or two days for it to become rotten, so it was continuously examined by the inspector right through from the delivery to the cutters. It moved along the conveyor line at a fast pace. Many thousands of fish went along that conveyor, by the cutters and the canners.

The ladies were also under contract to the Chinese boss. The way they were paid was piecemeal for each small wooden tray they filled. There was a Chinese worker that had a hole puncher, and the lady had a coupon hanging over where she was filling the cans. The coupon was punched for every tray that had been filled. That coupon was the way they tallied the number of fish the lady had processed each day. Not all the ladies got the same amount of pay. Some were quite fast, and others were quite slow in filling the cans. I remember the look of all the arms and hands moving when the fish were being put into the cans. Once they were in the cans, the fish went onto another conveyor belt and into a steam box that had a tray, and when the tray turned over, the fish were put through the steam box and moved along out to the other end, where they came out after being steamed. The steam box was more to preserve the fish.

Some days, and especially on the weekend, they got overloaded with fish at the cannery. The fish started to get rotten and smelly, so the Chinese boss stopped the operation right there, and let the fish going through the conveyor lines be finished off, getting the lids on the cans after they were steamed, and from there into a cooker, which finished cooking the canned salmon. From there, it was brought out to cool off and then boxed ready for shipment to the packing houses or the storage houses in Vancouver.

I worked until the cannery closed at the end of June, when the fishing season ended. At that time I went to the Chinese boss, and he wrote out my payroll statement. He handed it to me, and that was the end of the first job I had ever undertaken. I learned that whatever job you take, you don't quit, because that's where your knowledge of how other people make a living comes from, and how the labour system works in the fishing industry. I saw where the fish came into the place of delivery, where the fish packers came in who had collected fish from the fisherman, the ones who were fishing out on the channels and the ocean where the fish were coming in. I didn't experience the fishing the first year. My brother experienced the fishing part, I got the cannery.

So, I come to what happened on my first payday. I handed my pay — 13 dollars in cash — over to my aunt. She demanded that she should hold my money until she was ready to give it to me, when I needed something, to use it wisely. That was my aunt's purpose for taking my money. She tied it in a sock and hid it somewhere. I didn't know where she had it hidden, even though we were travelling in a small boat. Then we travelled back to our homeland, and eventually I went back to the residential school. I told my friends in the school that I had been working all summer and that I was broke already! My aunt let me spend my money buying a shirt and socks and underwear, which left me completely broke by the time I returned to school.

Most of the children left the residential school at the age of 16 years. Many went into the fishing industry, which needed experienced people to work in places like Rivers Inlet, at the Good Hope Cannery. In Rivers Inlet there were approximately 12 canneries operating, and they were all using the same techniques as at Good Hope, most of them using Chinese labourers. My thoughts concerning the Chinese labourers, and my thoughts still today, are that it was a very poor income. What they got paid was not enough to make a living. But what else can you do? It was one of the first industries that went into heavy operation, making jobs for young people and Chinese labourers and the fishermen.

During those early years I remember there was a Japanese company that put up what were called "salteries," because at the time there was no other way to preserve the salmon. Because of the richness in the sockeye, coho, and spring salmon, these fish seemed to decay and spoil within one day in the open. Consequently, there was much wastage at various canneries because of overfishing at the height of runs. Fish simply could not be processed fast enough.

Fishboats off Ahousaht on the outer side of Flores Island, about 1950.

One of the Ahousaht fishboats, possibly Harold Lucas's troller.

After 20 or 30 years had passed, they shut down all the canneries at Rivers Inlet and moved them closer to the big city, to Steveston. There was one cannery left in operation, called Namu Cannery, and it still did the same type of work, the same type of canning, and needed the same type of fishing knowledge. They did change from gill-netting to seining, though. Seining is a more profitable method of fishing for salmon. As far north as the Nass River, and all along that route, there were canneries operating. It was the end of the canneries on the southern coast, though.

I went from the job at the cannery to working on a seine boat. All jobs aren't exactly the same, but what they do is give you experience. You learn that you should do a good job, no matter what faults the job has. From this job, I went onto a seine boat in the following summer, as a teenager around 14 years of age. I learned many new tricks of the trade working on a seine boat. At that time, it seemed like very heavy work, long days, frequently getting soaking wet. One difference was that the skippers on the boats were very cranky, using bad language, and criticizing how you worked. So, I learned that all jobs have something wrong, which is an unhappy situation. The seine boats were much different than working in the cannery, but they gave me valuable experience running a boat.

There were some years when I had a boat for myself. One of my boats sank offshore in foggy weather at night. Another boat had rammed us, but we all survived. Those are the sorts of things that you experience being at sea, working and fishing. In some of the years I experienced hardship, heavy losses, and financial problems in the costs of operation. Still, I learned all the time from this work, and I am not sorry that I experienced it.

More on Growing Up

The fish canneries played an important role for us as they caused a major change in our pattern of living. Throughout the 1920s, 1930s, and 1940s, the life of the Nuu-Chah-Nulth people was uprooted, causing many different cultural "breaks"; I call them breaks because the changes were so different, so diverse.

Commercial fishing has dominated our search for salmon in the past 60 years or so. I would like to stress that this change in something so important to our lives influenced everything we did. My memories of this go back to the mid-1930s, of how this change influenced us. In the fall season, the chum salmon, coho, and spring salmon came to the rivers and channels in Clayoquot Sound, Millar Channel, Russell Channel, and Father Charles Channel from the open Pacific. In early times there were no buyers or no commercial fishing. The early 1930s saw some commercial fishing ventures, for example the selling of fish by First Nations

Canadian Pacific's coastal steamer *Princess Maquinna* and the *Loyal*.

Fishboats from the west coast, mostly from Tofino – "a fortune in boats."

people to the local buyers — in particular, the two residential schools, in Ahousaht on Flores Island, and at Kakawis on Meares Island. Chum salmon and cohos were sold for about four cents apiece. It was not until the mid-1930s that BC Packers, Nelson Brothers, Francis Millard and Sons, and a few other companies started the industry going in our waters. The industry then created a demand, although the price of the fish was very low.

For our fishing and sea travel, First Nations travelled in dugout canoes, 24-foot motor boats, the one-lungers, 30-foot one-lungers. More recently they moved to modern-equipped fishing boats for trolling and gillnetting and seining. Our people adapted to the change as the various new industries came into existence. I can remember my father showing me how the one-lunger was operated and how to turn the flywheel over and start the motor. I learned how to take a boat out by myself while I was quite young.

Fish and forests were always important to the First Nations people. We worked both in our traditional ways and in the

Spirit of Marktosis, delivered from boat builders on the Fraser River. When it was finished, Earl brought it up to Ahousaht and skippered it for a couple of years; it is still running as a sea bus.

The late Walter Campbell, a kind-hearted and smart young man, with halibut, together with Wesley Thomas (Ahousaht).

industries that moved into our territories. As a young man I also worked in the logging industry. There too I experienced some of the changes in logging through my years of working in the forest. The story of my experiences begins as a 16-year-old residential school graduate from Ahousaht. I was looking around for some kind of work to make a living. I decided to wander away from my village because there was no employment there and to move to Port Alberni, where I had friends and could look for employment in the lumber mills.

I was hired first on a part-time basis at Bloedel, Stewart and Welch as an ordinary labourer. I was put on the nightshift, piling the heavy timbers as they came out from the mill. I learned how to operate and manoeuvre them by using a levering tool called a peevee. I was a youngster and the work was heavy, the hours were long, and the noise was terrible. Throughout the night I could hear the saws screaming in my ears, but I had to make a living. Fortunately, I found a friend and relative up the Somass River near Port Alberni, Adam Siwish, hereditary chief of the Tseshaht Nation, who asked me to move in with his family. Actually it was his father, Jacob, who asked his son to find me somewhere to stay while I was working at the mill until I could find a place for myself.

Adam Siwish was a very generous and kind young man. He brought me down to talk with the hiring people where I found work. When I say generous, I mean he was more than generous because he already had several families living in his house. I felt like I was encroaching because I had one room to myself. And every morning when I came back from the mill, he would offer me breakfast and I would sleep during the day. They would let me sleep throughout the day until I got ready to go back on shift. For one day of work, I was paid $5. And out of this I had to pay my room and board, and buy my working clothes. It took a while to sort myself out. After a month of work, I decided that I was imposing on the big family of Adam Siwish, although they assured me otherwise, and that I could stay as long as I wanted.

I was following Blind Dan's advice in going to Port Alberni. I hung around and worked there for some time in order to get travelling money. Down on the waterfront was a train station. Trains were the only way to go at that time. There was no bus service. In the beginning of June, there was a lot of activity down at the station. There were tents pitched and a fire started to cook meals, tea and bread. That was actually the main meal for the people living around there. If somebody happened to bring in a fish, they put the fish into a pot and it became boiled fish stew.

Salmon, meat — deer meat, hair seal, fur seal — and bannock were all important. People moving about don't have a proper kitchen, but it wasn't hard to make bannock. We call it Indian bread. It's cooked in many ways. Even on a sandy beach all you need to do is build a fire and put the bannock dough under the sand, where it will cook. When it gets cooked, you just shake off the sand and it's ready for eating. You can cook a fair-size loaf of bannock, enough to put in your two hands. You break it up into pieces, and you're able to eat as much as you want. Just flour and water and baking powder, nothing fancy. You carried your flour around with you; you'd get a sack of flour, a 20- or a 10-pound sack. Most stores kept it in different-sized sacks in order for people to buy the amount they needed when they were in one place. Then they'd move on and find another source, somewhere on their travels.

After I had worked at the mill in Port Alberni for a while, I asked the management at the mill during my off hours if I could find work in the woods and learn how to take logs out of the bush, or find some different kind of work as a logger. They arranged a transfer for me to go from the mill to a logging camp at Great Central Lake.

After seven months at the logging camp, I went over to Seattle looking for work. Moving to the American side and hiring out from Archie's hiring hall in Seattle, I was sent up into the Cascade Mountains, 45 miles outside of Seattle, to a camp that was sitting on railroad tracks. In fact, when I went up to the camp, I rode up on what they called a "crummy" on the railroad track. Everything was placed on that railroad track sitting against the mountain quite high up in the Cascades. It was summer, 1942, when I moved into the bunkhouse there.

In Great Central Lake, I had been a whistle punk. My job was to stand on a stump and listen for the signals coming from where the cutting was going on and to signal the riggers to pull logs out from the bush. There was the choker man, who wrapped the steel cable around the log and snapped it into the choker so that the log could then be yarded out of the bush. The rigging slinger helped the choker man and gave him orders for which logs to take out to the line where rigging was coming from. There was also a head-rigger, who stood by and made sure that the crew was working properly. It was the choker man who told the rigging slinger when it was time for the yarder to get into operation and haul the logs up the slope.

There was a main line which hauled the logs in from the woods and there was a line which was called a haul-back, the haul-back bringing the rigging. The rigging could be set anywhere along a road, but usually the logs were started from the closer end to the yarding machine which in those days was a gas engine with a winch and cables that wound in either the mainline or the haul-back line. The rigging was set out from the yarder, which was tied down to stumps so that it would hold when the yarding started from the bush.

I found a very different system on the American side, because the logging crew was actually two sets of crews. One was called the rigging crew and the other the operating logging crew. The difference was that one crew was setting up the rigging on the one road while the operating logging crew was yarding logs uphill on another line. And it was called a skidder show, the skidder being machinery up on top of the hill where the logs are being yarded up. And when they reached the top, they were dropped to the ground and the rigging went back downhill to pull up more logs.

I will just say that the Cascade Mountain rigging caused heavy damage to the sidehill because the logs had to be dragged on the ground with their tail ends, ten at a time, scarring the sidehill, knocking and uprooting everything that went in their way. There is no really safe, easy way of not hurting the forest lands when you're harvesting this type and number of logs. As the rigging moved from one site, when this road was finished, the logging crew moved onto the next row. This was in turn moved, going right around the mountain in the kind of way that the train moved as the logging progressed and the logs were harvested and loaded onto the train.

I am outlining this to explain how the rigging and cables worked to drag logs from the bush anywhere from 400 to 500 yards distant from the machine. Three to four chokers at a time were hanging from the rigging. I remember the damage that it caused was tremendous because the logs destroyed anything that was in their way. The damage from where I saw it, standing on a stump, included pulling the salal bushes, huckleberry bushes, and other small plants in the path; all would be yarded out. It seemed that the earth itself would crumble under the pressure of the logs.

There is no real way of compensating for, or repairing, the damage that is done on one road and in one clearcut because the early machinery was not made to lift these heavy logs off the ground. This is my early experience. I ask myself, what did it do to my mind? I was 16 years old and living during a time of very different attitudes, with loggers who sweated and worked and pulled these logs out of the bush.

After working in the Cascade Mountains, I logged in various other camps on the American side. In 1945, I returned to British Columbia, an experienced young man, having served in the armed forces during World War II, looking for a job. My next job was in the logging camp at Tahsis on Nootka Sound, up the coast of Vancouver Island. At Tahsis, I worked at the loading works at Strange Island. The system was very different because the logs were being loaded onto gutted-out sailing vessels, the *Tolmie* and the *Malahat.* They had cut out the deck and beams on both ships so that logs were loaded down into the bottom of the ship. The machinery for loading logs onto the two vessels was powered by very old steam engines fired by wood, so that when the logs were lifted the engines would steam. It would take some time for the steam to build up in order to lift in some more.

Both of those vessels eventually sank in heavy weather. The

Landslide damage in Clayoquot, a result of logging; note person in the centre.
HERB HAMMOND

Malahat was being towed off Barkley Sound when it hit bad weather and foundered. They towed the wreck to Uchucklesit Inlet where the old ship was abandoned for a time, but later it was moved to Powell River where the sunken wreck is now. The *Tolmie* was also lost, so all the logs that were on these vessels drifted and were lost (or log salvagers got them), proving a heavy loss for Gibson Brothers logging company, who owned them.

At that time the logging operations at Tahsis were six miles up the Tahsis River. It was one of the places where I found early evidence of environmental damage to the fish stream. Logs were dragged by a bulldozer along the riverbed. For many years, the operation used the river as a road. And there was a dump at the bottom end of the river where the logging truck dumped its logs. The road was the river, so that anything that went downstream went down the river.

Today we call the river and its shorelines a "hydro-riparian

Sulphur Passage, near Shark Creek, site of roadblock to protest MacMillan Bloedel logging. NANCY J. TURNER

zone," and we now seem to understand the importance of these areas. The Tahsis sockeye and chum runs were pretty well ruined by that logging. And you can imagine what little is left there now after over 50 years of operation.

I have seen what the logging companies do, and how they act. They wanted to do the same in the lands in Clayoquot Sound that I inherited all the way back from Maquinna. A few years ago we set up a roadblock just on the road not far from Shark Creek on Sulphur Passage, about a quarter of a mile from where road blasting was going on. There were many reasons why we blocked the work of the logging company at this site. First off, this was traditional Ahousaht territory and I, as chief, decided to protest the logging of all the areas along that side of the channel on the Vancouver Island side, Shark Creek and Atleo River, called Seektukis, the main river of the Ahousaht.

Atleo River was a very rich salmon river, but I can say now

Clearcut, Clayoquot Sound, 1993. NANCY J. TURNER

that the stream is damaged due to the heavy impacts from the logging practices of MacMillan Bloedel (now bought out by Weyerhaeuser) and Fletcher Challenge (now TimberWest) and other logging companies that have operated in that area on the northwest side of Millar Channel. I am not the owner, but I am the keeper of Shark Creek. I am the person who watches and sees that no damage is done to Shark Creek. As I said before, it is called Mamach-aqtlnit because the basking sharks had their young at the deeper part of the pool below the waterfall on the saltwater side of the tidal pool. And this sacred pool is shared with my family.

How I have responded to my people's recollections and my own experience has formed my view of the future. A good part of the future is linked to the treaty negotiations we are now undertaking with the governments of British Columbia and

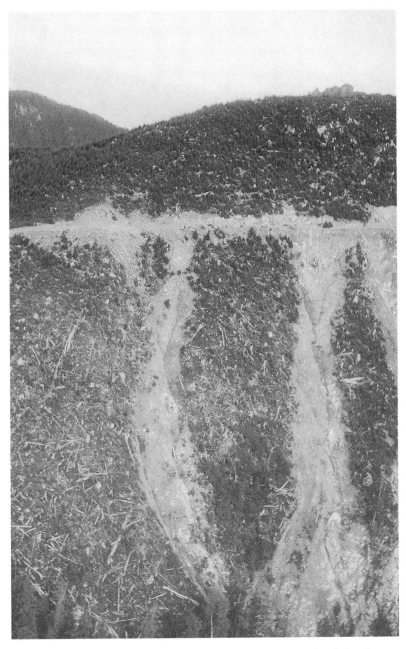

Landslides resulting from logging and road construction, Sand Creek, Clayoquot Sound, 1993. NANCY J. TURNER

View of Clayoquot Sound from Flores Island. NANCY J. TURNER

Canada. My ancestors have captured great whales, they and I have hunted the fur seal, I have fished and logged in many areas of First Nations territories. In the short period of a little more than a century, we have gone from using these things for our survival to being employees of large companies. We are now trying to regain some of what was ours so that we can survive with the food from the sea and also have work for our young people. Thus we sit at the treaty table and try to settle the issues of land and resources with the Crown. That is the focus of the next chapter.

HaHuulhi
and *Traditional Territories*

I have been thinking about land.
This is what the whole treaty is about.
Essentially, they came and took our land away.

THE PURPOSE OF THIS PART OF THE BOOK is to give a message to my grandchildren, my children, and family of the *Ha'wiih* (hereditary chiefs) of Ahousaht. I refer to the question of settling ownership issues over land and sea, rivers, and streams with all the European nations that came and settled in British Columbia and who did not respect the First Nations in Clayoquot Sound. What I have written is a very short examination of the inequities that we are trying to resolve on the treaty table. I begin this chapter with the story of how our song of prayer to the Thunderbird, Tiskin, was given to us. I then place the song in its current setting, the treaty negotiations — our first and only such deliberations. We know we are facing very hard negotiations as to what the two governments have to offer, because each of them has different ways of dealing with the matters that are their responsibility. I will use a chronological framework to discuss the progress of the negotiating process.

Our negotiations are not carried out by themselves so I discuss some of the outside issues that have influenced our thinking on the treaty and may also influence the government negotiating position as well. My source for this material is from legend passed down to me from my ancestors, and from my position as one of the Nuu-Chah-Nulth treaty negotiators. I can only think that, by seeing some of the provincial government's attitudes and "democratic" ideas, they are different from an aboriginal person's mind, such as mine. To understand the meaning of aboriginal rights of First Nations is to allow them to live the way they lived before the coming of the settlers and the laws that came first under the British North America Act.

The Song of Tiskin

There is a song we sing at the beginning of every treaty meeting. This song is about the strength of Tiskin, almighty Thunderbird. It dates back to the generations before the wars between the Ahousaht and Otsosat Nations. It came as a spiritual awakening to two warriors (one an ancestor of Blind Dan's) who were

Left to right: Cliff Atleo, Earl George, Nelson Keitlah, Stanley Sam, Robert Thomas, Bill Kietlah Jr., Jimmy Swan, Shawn Atleo, Cosmos Frank, Edgar Charlie, and Louie Frank – all from Ahousaht.

preparing to avenge the killings of their chiefs. One was called Betokamai, and the other, Totohsata. These two were preparing to kill Kaanaqim. He was a dictator and a commoner using his power and strength alone, who had killed most of the Ahousaht Nation *Ha'wiih* and threatened the other chiefs enough to become the chief by the power of his wickedness. Kaanaqim was a giant that had been born to the ordinary people of the Ahousaht Nation

 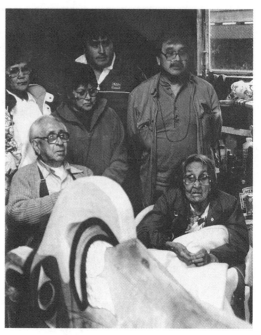

Josephine's father, Joseph Smith, from Queen's Cove – Ehattesaht (Zeballos originally).

Joseph Smith and Josephine's grandmother Xweena, Walter Michael's mother from Zeballos, Tim Paul (Josephine's son) (centre back), Josephine's younger brother, Earl Smith (back right), and others unidentified.

before the wars. His arms were twice the size of an ordinary person's. He had seven sons and a wife who was very wicked. Kaanaqim had one more hereditary chief to kill in order to hold the total chieftainship of the Ahousaht Nation.

Betokamai and Totohsata had gone to Nu-a-suk (Bartlett Island) to prepare to conquer Kaanaqim. They prepared themselves on the island for two years, training and praying that they would be able to kill Kaanaqim. Kaanaqim himself used to visit them. He knew that the two warriors were preparing to avenge the killings of their chiefs. He'd go to Nu-a-suk, and would enjoy just being

Earl's son Corby, who has taken over the chieftainship duties.

a guest. He'd say, "Aren't you afraid of what I did to so-and-so? He's not here anymore." Not only that, they'd treat Kaanaqim as a guest, giving him what they had on the table. Kaanaqim was treated like a king. But deep inside him, he was a wicked person. He would say, "I'll be the head *Ha'wiiha* after I finish you off."

Once he went out to Nu-a-suk and met the two warriors talking together on the water in their canoe. They were far enough away from Kaanaqim that they were not going to harm each other. Kaanaqim taunted them, saying, "I'll kill you both before you try to kill me. I invite you both to try what you are planning to do, to kill me, but you will go out of my house as corpses. I welcome you to try. There's no man stronger than Kaanaqim," he said of himself.

Tiskin, the Thunderbird, came to these two warriors with the song. It is the same song that was passed on through the generations to me, that I have now given to the Nuu-chah-nulth Tribal Council as a means of being successful in the fight to keep our *HaHuulhi*, our rights to our traditional territories. This song is what we are using now to pray that the Thunderbird is going to use its strength in order to give us back the resources and land in Clayoquot Sound we once owned. So it is the song the Thunderbird first sang to the two warriors.

The warriors eventually succeeded in killing Kaanaqim after their second year of praying on Nu-a-suk. They went to his house on the Cypre River, where he lived with his seven sons. Kaanaqim told his sons, "You just keep your distance on the sides because I'll kill the two warriors with my own strength, myself." Kaanaqim's nephew was standing beside him, holding his club. Kaanaqim had another club that he was prepared to use, but it was for the last part of his fight, the killing of the two warriors. So his sons obeyed him and stayed on the sides waiting to see from which side the two warriors would enter the fight. Kaanaqim was standing near the centre of the house while the two warriors were making ready to fight. His nephew was standing behind him and he said to his nephew, "Give me my better club." He was facing towards the centre of the room, where the two warriors were ready to fight. But, instead of handing him his club as he was commanded, his nephew took it and clubbed Kaanaqim from behind, killing him instantly. The sons standing on the side did not move. They were awestruck to see their father die. Kaanaqim was finished, at the hand of his own nephew.

That is when the song of the Thunderbird was sung by these two warriors, Betokamai and Totohsata. The song has been passed down through the generations, to my grandfather, Chief Billy, and then to my father, and over to me. Now it is in the hands of the Nuu-chah-nulth Tribal Council. That song is sung first thing before every meeting at the treaty table. It is what we believe is going to spell victory for the Nuu-Chah-Nulth Nation.

Our Lands

I have been thinking about land. This is what the whole treaty is about. It is about how the land changed from First Nations territories with the coming of the settlers, those people who came and imposed their sovereignty over us. Essentially, they came and took our land away.

The Province has a way of holding on to land, naming it Crown land. The settlers call their landholdings "fee simple" land. Around the turn of the century, the lands in Clayoquot Sound were divided up by a royal commission. The commissioners came to the area, telling the Nuu-Chah-Nulth people to put a stake at the end of their dwellings, and all the tribes put up survey posts. Then they were told, "This is the land you are going to live on, reserve land." These lands amounted to little fragments of property where our people were dwelling at that particular time, "given" to us, although the federal government retained ownership to the land. At the time we may not have clearly understood the whole process. We now understand very well the meaning of naming these lands that the settlers took as their private lands.

One such site we held on to is a special island where the First Nations meet, called Nu-a-suk. We are not one tribe, but a confederacy of the First Nations like Keltsomaht, Ahousaht, Manhousaht, Quaswiaht, Ouinmitisaht. There was a shelter at Nu-a-suk where you could land on the sand beach, even on a day of very rough surf. Although white people had no knowledge of the place, we were required to stake it as a reserve. The settlers did come as far as another site, Tofino, Grice Point (*Nachiks* in our

Earl's daughter, Grace George.

language), which belonged to the Nuu-Chah-Nulth who were dwelling there. *Nachiks* is a word which means that you can see across to another village, which was Opitsat on Meares Island. We were not able to keep that site, and now it is being developed as a prime tourist destination after spending most of its life as a quiet fishing village.

Ahousaht women dancers; Evelyn Atleo (second from left), with Myrtle Samuel next to her.

Stanley Sam and young Ahousaht dancers in a recent photo.

January 1996: The Framework Agreement

The negotiation now before us represents the final act of our past relationship with European people. In 1995, the chief negotiators were appointed by each of 12 nations of the Nuu-Chah-Nulth that are participating in this process. One First Nation, Ditidaht, chose to meet Canada and British Columbia independently, and since that time other Nuu-Chah-Nulth nations have chosen to withdraw from the treaty process. For the Ahousaht, there are two of us that sit at the table, and both of us have the authority to speak. Most of the Nations have one chief negotiator. The four northern Nuu-Chah-Nulth nations appointed one chief negotiator for all four tribes.

So there is variation in the people sitting around the treaty table. There are three co-chairs designated as chief negotiators for all the 12 Nuu-Chah-Nulth nations: Nelson Keitlah, Lillian Howard, and Richard Watts. The governments came with negotiators appointed at the federal and provincial levels. Throughout 1995, the Nuu-Chah-Nulth were negotiating the framework agreement to outline all of the aspects of our aboriginal lifestyles to be recognized by both federal and provincial governments as part of the negotiating process.

In January 1996 there was a letter from Wendy Porteous, chief negotiator for the Government of Canada, directed to Murray Rankin, treaty negotiator for the Province of British Columbia, and provided to co-chairs Nelson Keitlah and Richard Watts and to Victor Pearson, our treaty manager who keeps track of all the business throughout the talks with both governments. Although regulations preclude me from revealing the full contents of the letter, it provides the details of the system for modern treaties. The letter says that parties to the treaty are there due to a political commitment to negotiate but that no party is legally bound to participate. The letter was careful to note that this first stage, the framework agreement, did not create a legally enforceable right.

The framework agreement is very important, because when we get into the agreement-in-principle, the next stage, some issues will not be easily understood by some people because they may not be within the history of experience of some First Nations people. For example, as I discussed earlier, few outsiders would be aware of the role of fur seals and the fur seal industry in our lives. Seal hunting for subsistence, for example, is still an aboriginal right protected by the Constitution of Canada, although no one has tested that right in recent years.

A draft framework agreement between Canada, British Columbia, and the Nuu-chah-nulth Tribal Council has been written. At that point we had not initialed it, and thus not agreed to the framework agreement, but the papers were set in place. There was a Nuu-chah-nulth Tribal Council meeting on January 12 and 13, 1996. Our discussions suggested that some tribes were ready to sign and some others were not, but it seemed that overall we were not ready. Our lack of readiness was and is due in part to the changing fabric of the framework agreement. We wished to see issues in the agreement that the governments were not prepared to discuss at that point.

A key issue for us in the framework agreement addressed the residential school situation. The federal government especially did not want to discuss the schools in the framework agreement while there were court cases pending regarding the residential schools. Many individuals who spent their youth in a residential school have come forward and related terrible events that happened during their years there. We believe this to be a problem integral to the framework agreement. We were particularly taken aback by this issue because of the recollections of cruelty and abuse of our people and those of other First Nations in remote villages up and down the coast. However, the federal government has only recently begun to accept the legitimacy of the reports of the events.

A second broad issue relates to Crown land activities and aboriginal rights. Recent court decisions, such as the Sparrow decision, redefined the legal relationship between the Government of British Columbia and aboriginal peoples. The Sparrow decision was brought to the Supreme Court of Canada on May 31, 1990. The Supreme Court of Canada rendered its decision and recognized that the Musqueam First Nation, and by extension other aboriginal peoples, had unextinguished aboriginal rights to fish for food, ceremonial, and societal purposes. These rights were held by the collective, in keeping with our culture. The governments may justify activities that may infringe on any aboriginal right protected under section 35 of the Constitution Act, 1867, by meeting the principles established by the Supreme Court of Canada and reaffirmed with the results of the Sparrow case. In March 1993, the provincial Minister of Environment, Lands and Parks, in response to this decision, issued interim guidelines on aboriginal use of fish and wildlife. The Sparrow decision is important to treaty negotiations because the aboriginal rights were proven to be still in place and protected by the Constitution.

There are seven other decisions rendered at the same time by the British Columbia Court of Appeal that dealt with aboriginal people on a variety of issues, including hunting and fishing rights. As I write this, I expect more and more cases to come through the courts. The implications of these decisions are significant, and they are effectively changing the nature of the legal relationship between the Province of British Columbia and First Nations. Aboriginal rights continue to exist in British Columbia. They may vary from context to context in accordance with distinct patterns of historical occupancy and use of land. An activity in question must have been in existence prior to 1846, and over a sufficient length of time to become integral to the aboriginal society.

In order for the Province to engage in any activity on Crown land, it should make its best efforts to first determine if aboriginal rights exist in the area and if the proposed provincially sanctioned activities will infringe upon those rights. If it is determined that an activity does infringe upon aboriginal rights, that infringement should be avoided where possible, unless it can be justified pursuant to the principles established by the Supreme Court of Canada and the Sparrow decision. How this is dealt with in various jurisdictions, however, can be quite different.

February 1996: Other Resource Issues

While treaty negotiations were underway, there were other processes that had been developed due to court decisions. An important interlocking process for the First Nations of the central areas of Clayoquot Sound is the Central Region Board. This board is meant to establish some joint authority over resource management and put an agreement to work that will be the foundation for resource management in the final treaty. The Central Region Board (CRB) and the Province established the first interim measures agreement (IMA), "the framework within which the Province is approaching the land and resource component of treaty negotiations with First Nations." It was originally in force until March 19, 1996, and was extended.

I have sat on the CRB as a representative for Ahousaht. The land and resource issue is one of our foremost concerns, especially dealing with Tree Farm Licence 44, currently in corporate hands, but now bound by the Clayoquot Scientific Panel recommendations for sustainable forest practices, through another government process.

The CRB believes its objectives for planning, management, and cultural values are addressed through the Clayoquot Scientific Panel, but the government's and MacMillan Bloedel's [now Weyerhaeuser's] acceptance of the panel recommendations seems to require detailed amendment. If an agreement can be reached with government on the board's planning proposals, we will promote specific obligations for local economic benefits, such as employment for First Nations and other communities, and the retention of fiber in Clayoquot Sound to promote community businesses and to generate employment in local processing. This is a very positive idea that First Nations support because it helps us and our neighbours much more than the corporate approach to resource management.

We have an IMA in place, and we also have an understanding to co-manage in the agreement, a real chance for joint stewardship. The lifetime of the IMA should be longer. Politics seem to be a roadblock in the progress of the ideals of the IMA. My mind is bothered with the politics of the people in power, who seem to me to try to disregard the whole issue of aboriginal rights when discussing actually having to return some power to the original owners of the land.

November 1996: Sovereignty

Many issues are at hand in Clayoquot Sound, and there was an ongoing dispute between the Province and its Ministry of Forests, and First Nations of Nuu-Chah-Nulth tribes, Central Region: Hesquiaht to the north, Ahousaht to the south, and, further south, the Tla-o-qui-aht Nation, the Ucluelet and Toquot.

As of November 1, 1996, there was a vital issue that seems to be missing as talks proceed on issues regarding the agreement-in-principle. The Province of British Columbia claims: "at the time sovereignty was asserted in British Columbia, title of land in the Province became vested in the Crown." I state outright that any written documents that claim sovereignty by British Columbia were not properly permitted by the Nuu-Chah-Nulth nations. Having said that, I should add that, historically, the 14 tribes were at that time very sadly in a state of confusion. This issue has very recently been settled to a large degree by the Delgam Uukw decision. That ruling links aboriginal rights and title, and further gives respect to the First Nations way of holding land and resources.

A number of other court cases in recent years have held that the Crown's title is burdened by unextinguished aboriginal rights to lands and resources that formed a foundation for the larger decision. Together, the set of rights held by an aboriginal group is also sometimes referred to as "aboriginal title." For example, the Supreme Court of Canada in the Guerin case recognized "pre-existing aboriginal title" as a legal right other than one of ownership. In that case, the Indian agent allowed reserve lands to be removed for the higher purpose of building a golf course.

Early in the history of white peoples' occupancy we were confined to reserve lands and held as wards of the government, with one official from Indian Affairs for each First Nation under a system mandated by the Indian Act. So when they say "aboriginal title," they are only talking about the thin surface of aboriginal rights of people who were here for thousands of years before the arrival of the people who claim sovereignty in Canada and British Columbia.

As time goes on and treaty talks proceed toward an agreement-in-principle, we see and hear more of those people who are afraid that we will be given back the land that was essentially stolen from us. While the Province claims that the underlying title to land in British Columbia has never been questioned by the courts or by government, it certainly has been. They claim aboriginal rights do not supersede either Crown title or the "beneficial ownership" conveyed to the Province through the Constitution. The fact that aboriginal rights exist in British Columbia does not call into question the title of the Crown, but does create a legal burden on Crown ownership and management activities. On paper, the Province believes that fair and honourable treaty negotiations are necessary if these long-standing issues are to be resolved in a way that benefits all British Columbians. But I think sometimes the ideal of fairness does not have the same meaning between our two peoples.

For example, some third-party political structures, organizations, municipal governments, and federal and provincial bodies have shown very strong opposition to what has been settled with the Nisga'a people. I have read the Nisga'a Treaty which they have been fighting for through the courts and with governments for well over 20 years. I have the impression that the Nisga'a Treaty is not supported by the majority of white Canadians, but it has recently been signed and ratified.

April 1997: Roadblocks

As the spring was upon us, I had been thinking of the mandate of the government negotiators. I asked myself, "Is there a mandate?" They have no such thing as a mandate; rather it is what I call in my language "direction." We do have a lot of paperwork, two and a half to three years of paperwork for the Nuu-Chah-Nulth nations, but little else. The government will not say much on how things will be done as we proceed. Sometimes I seriously doubt that the government is capable of understanding its own way of regulating, let alone of understanding how we might manage ourselves. I can say I feel certain that we are beginning to be pushed over the edge again.

Our ideas about fish and streams and animals seem to be irrelevant to the treaty development, yet they are central to our way of thinking. We want to govern our own people, look after our own land, be our own stewards of what we have, what they've taken away. We want that back. We want to look after our own people and gain a sense of self-respect. It appears to me, based on the way negotiators talk to us, that the government does not believe we can take care of ourselves and our resources. Thus, no real progress has been made toward a settlement. I wonder if it ever can be so.

We were more and more going backwards at the time. We were monitoring what is being talked about around the tables with First Nations all across British Columbia. In all the negotiations that are ongoing, no talks have reached the agreement-in-principle stage. I feel safe in saying that governments were stalling the process before the Delgam Uukw ruling.

We have, in the last couple of meetings (around April 27, 1997) changed our way of treaty negotiations. This is because we were going too slow and we would not reach an agreement-in-principle, so vital to the treaty task. For example, an issue that has become laboured is access to land and resources by people on both sides of the agreement. Although "access" is a word which does not have proper meaning to me, it is being discussed at the negotiating table. Access will mean access to reserve lands, access to treaty lands, access to shared lands, and access to areas that are territorial lands. This became such a long, drawn-out issue that we decided we would hire a facilitator to give us more rapid answers to the issues of access so we could draft a position. So we hired a person called Daniel Johnson, a person who was recognized by the governments of British Columbia and Canada as a top-notch negotiator.

We had trouble using all the negotiators from the 12 Nuu-Chah-Nulth nations when all the negotiators sat around the main table. The trouble was that each nation would negotiate, and this resulted in the need for much draft paperwork to properly hear out each nation separately. Each nation would talk about the issues that were raised on the floor, and it would take one whole sitting to hear each issue.

So a motion was made by me to try a different style of negotiating, a different style of facilitating. We decided that using six negotiators to put together proposals for the agreement-in-principle would be more useful. The six negotiators are called the Tripartite Standing Committee (TSC). Even if one of the members was missing, the negotiations would carry on. I sat in on this committee as a witness, and also had the same powers to negotiate or advise if I disagreed with the discussion. The main table still has the power to decide how to deal with what has come out from the TSC. Even in this more flexible setting, I am not very satisfied with the attitude of the negotiators for Canada. In my judgment, Canada still wants to deal with First Nations in the same manner they have over the last 150 years, namely through their bureaucracies at Indian Affairs, through the mechanism of a band council. They have the full control of all these councils and, through them, any business that relates to administration and funding.

Canada seems unwilling to relinquish lands and resources to the rightful owners, calling these treaty lands. Treaty lands are those lands that belonged to our forefathers, and should by all rights belong to us in this day and age. And we want a settlement that will put the land back to the ownership of each of the Nuu-Chah-Nulth nations' territory, rivers, streams, and forests, into the rightful ownership of the Nuu-Chah-Nulth. So the intent of negotiations is still very dark. It is very disheartening because we are going to have to pay back 80 percent of the cost of the negotiations, and so far it has cost us a fortune, and we have not gotten anywhere near to finalizing and settling our treaty negotiations with Canada and British Columbia.

At several times in the negotiations, I have seen much to make me feel negative about the process. On the other hand, I would like to say that the people who are working on drafts relating to all the issues that are being negotiated have done a great job, documenting the information and recording the important parts of the treaty discussions. Very young people who are well educated have, to my mind, been pushing out the draft documents that are so much a part of a modern treaty. These people, who make up the working groups, the six negotiators, and the main negotiating table, are top-notch people who know full well what we are demanding of the governments of Canada and British Columbia. I have to give credit to every person who has put into perspective what needs to be recognized in the treaty between the First Nations of the Nuu-Chah-Nulth and the governments of Canada and British Columbia. Our people have done well. There is nothing that is missing. All issues have been talked about for the last two years, and the paper work is there. We don't want to be tied down anymore. We want to be our own government.

What I was talking about, the slowness, when I said that we were not getting anywhere, I was meaning that Canada and British

Columbia have not offered us anything at all to negotiate. What should happen, and what should happen fast, is that we should scrap the Indian Act and set up our own department, First Nations managing their own destiny through self-government. We are asking for the return of many of the things that were taken away from us by the governments that were formed at the time our lands were taken away. It is the right thing to do.

August 1997: A Reappraisal

Here are my own general recollections of sitting in as a hereditary chief and having the same powers as the head negotiators on the table. I have listened to the issues that were raised at the table and have been an observer on the Tripartite Standing Committee, which we are still evaluating. While there are many questions that we do not have the answers to, we do know that there is progress. I cannot gauge the progress until we receive answers from the other parties as to their willingness to put things down in an agreement-in-principle.

In the last sitting that we had (in the summer of 1997), they were asking the question, "Are you ready to talk about land selection?" So, what they're asking the negotiators is, "Are you ready to give us the maps and charts of where your land selections are in Clayoquot Sound?" And our answer to that is, "Yes we're prepared." We know already where our lands, rivers, streams, ocean are, all the area that we know is ours. A land selection process has now gone ahead.

We have an unwritten history well understood by advisors, *Ha'wiih* (hereditary chiefs), historians, families. Because this treaty is based on *HaHuulhi*, we know the areas that are owned by the *Ha'wiih* and are looked after by each family. Starting from the beach, we have what we call the beach owner. We know who owns all the beach in the front of each living area, we know who owns all the beach and foreshore out to the ocean fishing grounds, hunting areas, all around the whole area of Nuu-Chah-Nulth territory.

We also have unwritten and written boundary lines which are shared by neighbours on each side of the territory. We do not have any markings, but we do have names of the places where the boundaries exist. They are peaceful boundaries and we are not arguing exactly where each boundary is. The question the government asks is, "Where are your boundaries?" They have been told in court cases such as the Meares Island court case, also directly from us, where the boundaries are, and we do not change our minds as to the place and direction. More recently I was an observer to a ceremony between the Nuu-Chah-Nulth Nation and the Kwakwaka'wakw people over the settlement of a boundary dispute on Vancouver Island. We have demonstrated our ability to negotiate among ourselves, and I am confident that we will build a peaceful process to solve problems between First Nations.

We simply do not recognize any other nation in our territory, much the same as the government seems to feel. Only one of us was here first, and no war occurred to change the ownership of our land or transfer it to the newcomers. We hold this position that we do not agree with the system that was introduced, making certain areas Crown land, fee simple lands, private lands, parks,

Meares Island court case; Mary Hays (Tlaoquiaht) in centre. Dan David at far left (also Tlaoquiaht).

and offshore zones, without consulting First Nations.

All of this ties in with some things that are not agreeable to both governments. But we do know that to make a modern treaty, to make a settlement, these issues have to be resolved. What was settled when Confederation happened in Canada should have also included the governments of First Nations as well as the governments of Canada and British Columbia.

Here is an example of how we look at things from our position. One of the important issues we need to resolve relates to fisheries. It is a key issue for negotiating because of the many regulations for the conservation of fish. It also has many ties with other key issues, for example conservation and sustainability. We need fish; they are part of our territory.

A slightly different example comes from our view on timber.

Healthy fish stream in a diversely canopied riparian forest. HERB HAMMOND

It is one of the resource issues that is in the interim measures
agreement and is one of the questions that will form a bridge to
the agreement-in-principle as to part of the settlement that will
go to First Nations. The timber is standing in First Nations territory. Because of this it also bridges larger issues of control and
power involving how governments made some companies wealthy
by allowing them to have tree farm licences and full control over
the extraction of timber in Clayoquot Sound. This is one of the
issues in which we are claiming that we should have a share or
even part of what is left of the industry, and again, we see the
strong need for better protection of all the resources of Clayoquot
Sound.

First Nations are trying to participate in the management of
forests through the interim measures extension agreement, by
having the forest lands given back to First Nations in each territory
of Clayoquot Sound. We have much to say about forestry, not

Giant Douglas-fir near Shark Creek. NANCY J. TURNER

only for the trees and forest life but because it involves fish streams, salmon habitat of the watersheds in Clayoquot Sound.

A third area being discussed is wildlife: endangered, threatened, and vulnerable species. That is also a long-drawn-out issue that has broad implications. Earlier on, a whaling industry just about exterminated the great whales in our territorial waters in British Columbia, both by our own hunters and foreign hunters from around the world. It is one of the important issues to try to find a way to protect what is left of the life of the whale that was hunted on our coastline.

A fourth issue involves the question of water resource management in British Columbia. We were told by the Province that all water issues and the control of water rights are managed by the British Columbia government. They produced a paper called "Water Resource Management in British Columbia" (draft discussion paper for treaty table: May 1997), produced with no consultation with the First Nations or any understanding of our concept of ownership of water. Although it is a draft, it has issues and meanings and definitions and involves a moratorium on all water licences in British Columbia.

So this moratorium has to be reviewed and talked about at the treaty table to allow First Nations discussions and to examine the issue of drinking water and how people were given licences to bottle water and sell to the public drinking water which is from places and territories that belong to First Nations. We should have some form of power to manage and control our own drinking water and our own rivers and streams in our territories. Each of our places where we lived, even water wells and springs, had names. The names were usually quite understandable or known by all resident families living in our village sites. And all the streams have names, including the streams that run down the steepest mountainsides.

I touch here only briefly on some of the issues that are being raised at the treaty table and note that all of this is still in a draft and being used for discussion.

We could produce volumes and volumes on the injustices involving First Nations people in Clayoquot Sound, right from the time when the king and queen of England proclaimed sovereignty over British Columbia, Clayoquot Sound, and ignored the *Ha'wiih* and their *HaHuulhi* in Clayoquot Sound. I remember when an American military vessel lost a barge carrying equipment up to Alaska. The barge drifted ashore on Nu-a-suk (Bartlett Island), the meeting place of whaling chiefs. I want the reader to understand, and also my family to understand, the respect that was shown by the American military that came ashore to the people on Bartlett Island to pick up their barge. They asked for their barge and the answer was, "No, the barge has landed in the Nuu-Chah-Nulth territory of Ahousaht. You have to pay a cost to have your barge returned to you to take it off our territory." The American military awarded the *Ha'wiih* of the Ahousaht the fee to regain their barge in peaceful manner, recognizing and respecting the *Ha'wiih* of the Ahousaht. This is much more than the governments of Canada or of British Columbia have shown us.

So if you can sort out the injustice of these two instances — one, the instance of the American military recognizing the *Ha'wiih* of the Ahousaht nation, and the other being the kings and queens of England and Sir James Douglas not consulting the *Ha'wiih* of Clayoquot Sound as the sovereign owners of the Clayoquot Sound territory — you will be able to see a fraction of our frustration.

We would like to have the agreement-in-principle. And we are piecing together a document that will not be binding, but that will be changing in time when the young people take over the formation of government in Clayoquot Sound through the inheritance of *Ha'wiih* of all the nations of Nuu-Chah-Nulth. There are many substantive issues on hand and many documents, and each is being examined, talked about, and negotiated to bring justice to the nations of Nuu-Chah-Nulth, and to do away with the Indian Act, to remake our own government and our lives.

Editors' Note on the Treaty Process

Treaty negotiations between the Nuu-Chah-Nulth First Nations of Clayoquot Sound and the governments of British Columbia and Canada are still uncertain. The Nuu-chah-nulth Tribal

Council, representing 13 of its 14 member bands, entered the treaty process in January 1994 at a common treaty table with the non-member Pacheedaht First Nation. The Pacheedaht withdrew from the table in 1997 and joined the Ditidaht First Nation at a common table. The Hupacasath First Nation for Port Alberni withdrew from the treaty table in early 2000.

On March 10, 2001, chief negotiators for the Nuu-chah-nulth Tribal Council, British Columbia, and Canada initialled an agreement-in-principle. Each of the 12 participating bands developed a community consultation and approval process. Six bands, representing approximately two-thirds of the total population, rejected the agreement-in-principle, and six – including the Ahousaht by a slim margin – approved. Subsequently, on October 3, 2003, the Maa-nulth First Nations, comprising the Huu-ay-aht, Toquaht, Ucluelet, Uchucklesaht and Ka:'yu:'k't'h/Che:k'tles7et'h' (Kyuquot/Checklesaht), signed an agreement-in-principle with the Province and Canada. The remaining bands of the Nuu-chah-nulth Tribal Council, including the Ahousaht, continue to consider their options.

7

Conclusions

Ownership is based on what we call HaHuulhi. *It is not ownership in the white sense; it is a river or other place that is shared by all Nuu-Chah-Nulth people, with a caretaker being the hereditary chief of each site or village, such as Ahousaht.*

W<small>HAT</small> I <small>HAVE WRITTEN HERE</small> is part of a larger story. I could have said much more and related more stories. I wanted to do something that is not the same as what a historian would write, or an anthropologist, because I am neither. Although there is no discipline in a university in living as a First Nations person, what I have done is some inquiry into events surrounding my own life to try and present something that will help others understand what it is like to be a native person, at this time, and what kind of things at least one of us thinks about.

Earl and Josephine George enjoying each other's company during their 25th anniversary celebrations in the fall of 2002. ROBERT D. TURNER

Josephine George and Nancy Turner in 2002. ROBERT D. TURNER

Jaylyn Lucas enjoys drumming at a celebration to mark Earl and Josephine's 25th anniversary. ROBERT D. TURNER

We are concerned about our land, water, and the things that live there. We have a much closer relationship to those things; we have lived with them for thousands of years. We can see all through places like Clayoquot Sound that things now called resources have been very poorly managed. I worry that the forests and waters are being very seriously damaged. These are the things that have supported our people for all time and are part of our life.

We are, as you can see from what I have written, a sea people. In living by the sea and studying about it in university, I have many worries over the fish, seals, and whales. My ancestors had special relationships to the whales. Their protection or future hunting now seems out of our control. So, too, our knowledge of these animals does not seem to be of much interest to the current resource managers. That is why I wrote a chapter especially on the sea animals.

Clayoquot Sound, looking north towards Meares Island. NANCY J. TURNER

The book concludes with my thoughts on the stages of the negotiation process that I have participated in. This is not an analysis of the process or the content. It is my own observations and feelings as we went through the process of trying to iron out issues and move toward a settlement that will bring some foundation for the future of our people. Some parts may seem unfair, but I have put down my impressions as I felt them. Of course things may now change quite a bit due to the Delgam Uukw decision, but that is largely beyond what I am trying to accomplish here.

In this book I have written down many things that are part of my life as a First Nations person living through the last 76 years. Like many of my generation, I have lived through a time of great change. The stories of Maquinna were fresh in the minds of my grandparents, and the stories of Tiskin are as real to me as the stories of Christianity. The story of my own life, beginning in the residential school, seeing the end of sealing, and watching my people move in and out of various industries as the world changed around us, has been a lot to take in.

Much of what I say here is based on my own reflection. In negotiations people ask me, "What is the reason for your opinion?" What I have written here is the basis for my position. I sometimes try to find out what is the basis for the white people's opinion. When they say they want to do justice, I have a hard time understanding what they mean. It seems to me the white sense of justice is based on giving as little as possible. The treaty ideal of giving five percent of the land back to native people is supposed to be just. I think that giving back 100 percent of the land is maybe more just, especially of our homeland and traditional territory, like Clayoquot Sound.

It feels odd to have won the argument, yet not won an adequate settlement. As I have written here, and as the courts have now said, we have rights, and title. Our occupancy of the land and water and our stewardship of the resources is undeniable. That white people have taken the land and resources from us is also undeniable. I have watched while white people have taken more and more from the land and water that was once ours without so much as a "thank you."

That we are now negotiating is our choice, as an alternative to court action. We think we are being much more reasonable in the way we are seeking our land back than in the way it was taken from us. I cannot help but feel that the government and politicians are putting us on. Politics and justice here create a curious result.

Today, when we sit down with the governments of Canada and British Columbia, we talk about the many issues related to ownership. Ownership is based on what we call *HaHuulhi*. It is not ownership in the white sense; it is a river or other place that is shared by all Nuu-Chah-Nulth people, with a caretaker being the hereditary chief of each site or village, such as Ahousaht. After much discussion, *HaHuulhi* is now being recognized in the negotiations and has been identified and written into the framework agreement as one of the key issues, as accepted by the provincial and federal governments and the Nuu-Chah-Nulth nations.

Somehow the word "confederation" is used to describe our system of joint First Nation ideas of being many nations within a larger nation. For example, Francis Charlie's thoughts about being a Keltsomaht were that they were not an independent people; rather they were always tied in with the Ahousaht Nation, who lived on the outer side of the same island. It is a fitting description of how all nations should live, as we are all on different sides of the same island.

About the author

Chief Earl Maquinna George, M.A. ROBERT D. TURNER

Chief Earl Maquinna George, first hereditary chief of the Ahousaht First Nation of Clayoquot Sound on the west coast of Vancouver Island, was born in 1926 in the village of Maaqtusiis, on Flores Island. Chief Maquinna lost his mother when he was very young and spent his childhood years, until Grade 8, at the Ahousat Indian Residential School. He received traditional training from the elders at Maaqtusiis, as well as learning the skills of fishing and a sea-going life from his father, McPherson George. He also worked as a logger and with the Canadian Coast Guard, eventually earning his skipper's papers. He lost his first wife to illness, and later remarried, taking responsibility for two large families. He took on a major role in Nuu-Chah-Nulth treaty negotiations with the provincial and federal governments, and as an elder, began a university education, receiving a B.A. in history and an M.A. in geography from the University of Victoria. As well as chronicling Earl Maquinna George's experiences, this book offers a portrait of the issues and challenges facing aboriginal people in Canada. It explains, from a First Nations perspective, their deep attachment to their lands and resources and their long-standing quest for social and environmental justice.